CW00546886

Naval Aces of World War 1
Part 2

SERIES EDITOR: TONY HOLMES

OSPREY AIRCRAFT OF THE ACES • 104

Naval Aces of World War 1

Part 2

Jon Guttman

OSPREY
PUBLISHING

Front Cover
Oblt z S Friedrich Christiansen
was leading a three-aeroplane patrol
of Hansa-Brandenburg W 12 fighter
seaplanes from Zeebrugge naval
station on 15 February 1918 when,
at 1045 hrs, they sighted a large
Allied convoy being escorted by
two Felixstowe-based Curtiss H-12B
Large America flying boats. The
latter both fled, but upon being
overtaken at 1100 hrs, one of them
made a fight of it until the flying
boat was shot down in flames from
an altitude of 200 metres near Nord
Hinder lightship. Heavy seas
prevented the Germans from
landing near the wreckage, which
turned out to be H-12B N4338.
The flying boat's crew, Canadian
Flt Lt Claude C Purdy, Ens Albert D
Sturtevant, Boy Mech Arthur Hector
Stephenson and AM1 Sidney James
Hollidge, perished. Christiansen and
his observer shared the victory with
Flgobermt Urban and Ltn z S
Ehrhard.

Albert Dillon Sturtevant, an
officer of the US Naval Reserve,
was among the 29 members of
the First Yale Unit that had been
attached to Royal Naval Air Station
Felixstowe since October 1917.
The first American of any military
branch to die in aerial combat in
his own country's service during
World War 1, Sturtevant was
posthumously awarded the Navy
Cross and a US Navy destroyer was
later named in his honour (*Cover
artwork by Mark Postlethwaite*)

First published in Great Britain in 2012 by Osprey Publishing
Midland House, West Way, Botley, Oxford, OX2 0PH
44-02 23rd Street, Suite 219, Long Island City, NY, 11101, USA

E-mail: info@ospreypublishing.com

Osprey Publishing is part of the Osprey Group

A CIP catalogue record for this book is available from the British Library

ISBN: 978 1 84908 664 6
e-book ISBN: 978 1 84908 665 3
e-pub ISBN: 978 1 78096 414 0

Edited by Tony Holmes
Page design by Tony Truscott
Cover Artwork by Mark Postlethwaite
Aircraft Profiles by Harry Dempsey
Index by Alan Thatcher
Originated by Blenheim Colour Ltd, Oxford
Printed and bound in China through Bookbuilders

12 13 14 15 16   10 9 8 7 6 5 4 3 2 1

Osprey Publishing is supporting the Woodland Trust, the UK's leading woodland conservation charity, by funding the dedication of trees.

www.ospreypublishing.com

ACKNOWLEDGEMENTS
I wish to acknowledge the invaluable help provided by the following colleagues in the scavenger hunt for both information and photographs – Carl J Bobrow, Jack Eder, Colin Huston, Alex Imrie, Norman Franks, Jack Herris, Jörn Leckscheid, Stuart Leslie, Peter B Mersky, Colin A Owers, Ioannis Paloubos, Walter Pieters, Les Rogers, Gunnar Söderbaum, Aaron Weaver, Greg VanWyngarden and Thomas Zacharis. Posthumous thanks are also extended to Gottfried *Freiherr* von Banfield and Rear Adm David S Ingalls, whose collective recollections gave me a somewhat better understanding of the first air war as they experienced it. This book is dedicated to them and all their comrades-in-flight.

CONTENTS

SKY AND SEA

The application of aviation to marine matters well predates Austria-Hungary's declaration of war on Serbia on 28 July 1914. The American Civil War had seen both sides operate balloons from ships or towed lighters. When Louis Blériot flew across the English Channel on 25 July 1909, it served notice to the world – and in particular a nervous Great Britain – that bodies of water no longer constituted a protective barrier against the aeroplane.

Less than a year later an aeroplane had been developed that could operate from water, Frenchman Henri Fabre taking the first successful seaplane aloft in 1910. American Glenn H Curtiss built the first flying boat in 1912, and by 1914 seaplane tenders had been adopted by navies that saw the value of using these craft in support of fleet operations.

Wheeled aeroplanes were soon to join them. On 14 November 1910, American Eugene Ely flew his Curtiss Model D from an 83-ft wooden platform erected on the bow of the stationary light cruiser USS *Birmingham* (CL-2) in Hampton Roads, Virginia. Then in San Francisco Bay, California, on 18 January 1911, he landed aboard a 133-ft platform on the armoured cruiser USS *Pennsylvania* (ACR-4) using a tailhook to catch one or two of 22 ropelines, their ends weighted with sandbags, propped a foot above the deck. Fifty-seven minutes later, he took off again. The precedent for the aircraft carrier had been set.

It did not take long for navies to consider aeroplanes for a more malevolent purpose than merely the 'eyes of the fleet'. On 30 June 1910 Glenn Curtiss dropped dummy bombs on a battleship-shaped target in Lake Keuka, New York. On 27 July 1914 – just one day before war broke out in Europe – a British Short seaplane launched a 14-inch naval torpedo.

By then, other parties had already put theory into makeshift practice. During the Second Balkan War, on 6 February (24 January on the Greek Orthodox calendar) 1913, a Maurice Farman MF 7 seaplane crewed by Greek army 1Lt Michael Moutousis and navy Ens Aristeides Moraitinis made a 180-km flight over the Dardenelles in 2 hrs 20 min, during which time Moraitinis noted the presence of the anchored Turkish pre-dreadnought battleships *Torgut Reis* and *Hareiddin Barbarossa*, along with seven destroyers and three torpedo boats, at Nagara Point. He then dropped four grenades on the vessels. 'Three of the bombs fell into the sea', the Turks reported, 'and the fourth hit a field nearby a hospital, leaving a 15-centimetre hole in the ground'. Turkish troops fired back, but it was engine trouble that forced the Farman down in the Aegean Sea, where it was recovered and towed to Mudros, on Lemnos Island, by the Greek destroyer *Velos*. Moutousis' observer, Moraitinis,

The Maurice Farman MF 7 seaplane in which Greek army 1Lt Michael Moutousis and navy Ens Aristeides Moraitinis carried out a reconnaissance of the Dardanelles on 6 February 1913 is seen here being towed back to Mudros behind the Greek destroyer *Velos*. This flight climaxed in the first naval aerial bombing attack in history. Turkish gunfire failed to bring down Moutousis and Moraitinis, but engine trouble did, forcing them to land near Imbros – hence the need for a tow (*Hellenic Maritime Museum*)

would go on to be a distinguished pilot in World War 1.

In late May 1913, Didier Masson, a French-born naturalised American who had illegally entered revolution-torn Mexico with a Martin pusher so as to sell his services to the Constitutionalist army of Col Alvaro Obregón, dropped handmade bombs from an improvised rack fitted to his aeroplane on the 1880-ton federal gunboat *General Guerrero* in the Gulf of California. He made four attacks in as many days but failed to hit his quarry. Masson would subsequently return to France and fly with the American volunteer fighter *escadrille* N124 *Lafayette*.

By the time World War 1 broke out, navies as well as armies were adding aeroplanes to their arsenals. When Japan declared war on Germany on 23 August 1914, the entire air component available to the German garrison at Tsingtao, in China, was a Rumpler Taube flown by naval Kaptltn z S Günther Plüschow. Throughout the ensuing siege, Plüschow's lone reconnaissance sorties and occasional harassment raids using bombs made from coffee cans led to a concerted effort by up to nine Japanese army and navy aircraft to eliminate him. They did not succeed prior to the fall of Tsingtao on 6 November. Plüschow himself managed to flee and eventually make his way around the world, escaping from Chinese internment and imprisonment in Britain, to Germany, via the Netherlands, in July 1915.

As the concept of air superiority manifested itself over the Western Front in 1914-15, likewise did the matter of controlling airspace over the coastal regions become a concern among the combatant navies. This led to the development of fighter aircraft in parallel to the armies, although only Britain's Royal Naval Air Service (RNAS) would field fighters produced to its requirements. Designed by Sopwith, the 1½ Strutter, the Scout (aka Pup) and the Camel proved good enough to be adopted by the Royal Flying Corps (RFC) as well. Another, the Sopwith Triplane, did not, but it did see use with the French navy.

The other navies produced a smaller share of outstanding airmen who were credited with downing five or more opponents. The means by which they did so included not only landplanes, but also seaplanes or flying boats, some of which were designed for the fighter role. Ultimately, the German, French, Russian and Austrian navies organised fighter

Sonora was a Martin pusher acquired by Col Alvaro Obregón's Constitutionalist army in May 1913. It was fitted with improvised bomb racks and flown by Franco-American mercenary Didier Masson in four attempts to bomb the 1880-ton Mexican federal gunboat *General Guerrero* (*Smithsonian Institution 98-15481*)

Short Folder No 135, flown by Flt Cdr Francis E T Hewlitt, took part in an audacious ship-launched bombing raid by floatplanes against the Zeppelin base at Cuxhaven on 25 December 1914 (*Teral Research Services via Terry Treadwell*)

A Rumpler 4B 12 seaplane of the German *Kriegsmarine* flies a reconnaissance mission over the North Sea in 1915. As armed aircraft began to vie for control over the Western Front, a similar struggle escalated among the naval aircraft of both sides (*Private collection of Milosz Zielinski*)

An FBA (Franco-British Aviation) Type C flying boat of the French navy at CAM (*Centre d'Aviation Maritime*) Dunkirk, with British monitors in the background (*US Navy Historical Center NH 2584*)

components equipped with the same land-based fighters used by their respective armies. However, with the exceptions of one Greek and one US Navy pilot on temporary duty with the Royal Air Force (RAF), only the German *Kriegsmarine* could boast its own modest pantheon of aces who achieved that distinction exclusively in single-seat land-based fighters.

A Type UC II submarine passes by the mole at Zeebrugge. Allied efforts to neutralise the critically important U-boat base in the Belgian port led the German navy to establish air bases there and elsewhere along the Flemish coast (*Private collection of Milosz Zielinski*)

ZEEBRUGGE HORNETS' NEST

The Imperial German Navy operated seven seaplane stations along the southeastern shore of the North Sea during the war, and units based at four of them – Norderney, Borkum, Ostende and Zeebrugge – had frequent encounters with Allied aircraft. The most active, and notorious, facility of the lot was Zeebrugge, port to the city of Bruges. From here three aces would emerge.

After overrunning Belgium in August 1914, the Germans established stout defences at Zeebrugge, including a seaplane base formally designated as *Seeflugstation Flandern* (SFl) I on 4 December. Its first commander was Oblt z S Friedrich von Arnauld de la Perière, whose brother Lothar became the most successful submarine captain in history with 194 ships sunk totalling 450,000 tons.

Commencing operations from Zeebrugge mole on 17 December, the average of 30 seaplanes and flying boats that equipped SFl I would ultimately be credited with destroying 26 Allied aeroplanes, two airships, one submarine and six merchant ships, as well as a seventh vessel captured. Casualties by the end of September 1918 came to 27 personnel killed from all causes, four missing and 18 taken prisoner or interned in the Netherlands. The latter would include the CO, forced down by engine trouble in Friedrichshafen FF 33E Nr 493 on 17 December 1915, after which he and his observer, Ltn z S Hans Wirchow, were captured by the French. Oblt z S Bernhard von Tschirschky und Bögendorff replaced von Arnauld de la Perière in command.

The most famous of Zeebrugge's airmen, Bootsmannsmaat Friedrich Christian Christiansen, joined SFl I on 6 January 1915, and the next day he flew his first sortie in Friedrichshafen FF 29 Nr 204. Born in Wyk-auf-Föhr on 12 December 1879, Christiansen was the son of a sea captain and had served in the merchant marine – including a stint as second officer aboard the five-masted *Preussen*, the world's largest sailing ship – as well as the *Kriegsmarine* aboard motor torpedo boats in 1901-02. Taking an interest in aviation in 1913, Christiansen had earned Pilot's Certificate No 707 in March 1914 and was a flight instructor when called to war five months later.

Over the next two years Christiansen participated in a

Groundcrewmen at *Seeflugstation* I at Zeebrugge examine a badly damaged Friedrichshafen FF 33E, a mainstay reconnaissance seaplane for the base in 1916 (*Private collection of Milosz Zielinski*)

variety of patrols and bombing attacks, including a raid on Ramsgate on 9 February 1916. During an attack on Dover, with Kapltn z S von Tschirschky in the observer's pit, on 16 March, one of Christiansen's floats was punctured by anti-aircraft fire. The seaplane was then attacked by a British scout, which pressed home its attack to within 20 metres of the German machine. Von Tschirschky was hit in the shoulder and head and Christiansen in the thigh and hand. In addition, a valve rocker was shot off one of the engine cylinders and the radiator punctured. Christiansen managed to escape his attacker in a fog bank near Dean, landing in the water five miles offshore – unbeknownst to him amid a minefield!

Although he could hear British boats searching for him in the fog, Christiansen managed to repair his radiator, refill it with seawater and, with von Tschirschky perched on a float turning the propeller with his one good arm, restart the Mercedes engine. In spite of a leaking float that had his seaplane listing with one wing practically in the water, Christiansen took off amid a hail of fire from the now-alerted British search craft and returned to Zeebrugge some nine hours after his departure, and seven hours beyond his seaplane's endurance.

Christiansen was awarded the Iron Cross 2nd Class for his outstanding performance in the Ramsgate and Dover raids. He was also commissioned as a Leutnant zur See der Matrosen Artillerie and on 27 April 1916 he received the Iron Cross 1st Class and the *Ritterkreuz der Hohenzollern Hausorden mit Schwerten*.

Clashes with Allied aeroplanes increased. On 5 May 1916 FF 33H Nr 638, crewed by Oblt z S Kurt Reinert and Ltn z S Erich Bönisch, had an eventful patrol off Ostende in concert with unarmed floatplane FF 33E Nr 547 and the torpedo boat destroyer *V47*. The Zeebrugge station's war diary recorded the course of events as follows;

'At around 1130 hrs, seaplanes 547 and 638 took over the aerial defence of the destroyer that was working in the western part of the blockade area. At 1205 hrs two small cruisers and six destroyers were seen in square 066 Beta heading in an easterly direction at high speed. A report of this activity was immediately made to the torpedo boat destroyer *V47* and confirmation received that the message had been understood. At 1220 hrs an enemy seaplane was seen, and this was followed by 638 (crewed by pilot Oblt z S Reinert and observer Ltn z S Bönisch) to the vicinity of the enemy ships.

'As 638 turned away, a Nieuport fighting biplane was seen some 300 metres above and dead ahead. Both aircraft turned toward each other and the enemy opened fire at a range of 300 metres. The enemy aeroplane was hit by return fire and went down with its engine stopped and hit the water, whereupon it turned upside-down and sank. 638 descended to a height of 50 metres over the crash position, but a landing to rescue the enemy crew was no longer possible due to the proximity of the enemy destroyers.

'From statements made by two flying officers from a Short Seaplane that was captured the following day, it was learned that the body of the English Nieuport pilot had been picked up by an English ship. Our armed aircraft was supported during the fight by machine gun fire from *V47*, and our aircraft received some unimportant hits. However, due to an

Ltn z S Erich Bönisch was the first member of the German navy to be credited with five victories, albeit claimed from the observer's cockpit (*Colin Owers*)

over-heating engine it was forced to land on the water off Blankenberghe and was towed home.'

Reinert and Bönisch had downed a Nieuport 12 of 1 Naval Wing RNAS, the body of whose pilot, 24-year-old Flt Sub-Lt Herbert R Simms, was recovered by a British destroyer. It was later determined that he had drowned after the crash. His observer, Flt Sub-Lt Cyril J Mullens, was not found.

Bönisch was in FF 33H Nr 639 with Flgmstr August Ponater as his pilot on 8 June when they shot down a French Donnet-Denhaut flying boat near Thornton Bank at 1150 hrs. The crew, Quartier-Maîtres Henri Mercier and Le Prévost, of the Dunkirk-based *Centre d'Aviation Maritime* (CAM), were picked up by a U-boat and brought to Zeebrugge. On the 23rd of the month Friedrich Christian Christiansen, by now commissioned as a Leutnant zur See der Reserve, again saw aerial combat when he and Ltn z S Exner, in Nr 638, chased a Short Seaplane off with, they believed, heavy damage.

On 17 July Bönisch forged a productive working relationship with Flgobmt Karl Meyer when, flying FF 33H Nr 599, they brought down a French FBA flying boat. Born in Muhlhausen on 29 January 1894, Meyer had joined SFl I earlier that year. Flying FF 33H Nr 599 again, he and Bönisch shot down a Caudron G 4 behind Allied lines near Ostende on 2 August and, three days later, crewing Hansa-Brandenburg LW Nr 571, the two brought down another FBA off Middelkerke. This made Bönisch the first German naval observer to be credited with five victories.

On 31 August Ltn z S Niemeyer used a new single-seat seaplane fighter in the form of Rumpler 6B 1 Nr 751 to bring down a Short Seaplane, which landed near a destroyer. On 7 September he shot down one of 18 Caudron G 4s of 4 and 5 Naval Wings RNAS that were attacking St Denis Westrem, the aeroplane crashing north of Ostende and killing the crew. A second bomber was claimed by Meyer and Bönisch in Brandenburg LW No 571, but this was not confirmed – correctly, as the British only lost one G 4 in that raid. An FF 33H crewed by Ltn z S d R Soltenborn and Oblt z S Röthig forced a third Caudron crew to drop its bombs prematurely and flee.

Erich Bönisch's fighting career ended on 17 October when Brandenburg LW Nr 571 crashed, injuring him and his pilot, Ltn z S Hans Rollshoven. Six days later Niemeyer (in 6B 1 Nr 751) and Meyer (flying FF 33H Nr 820, with Flgmaat Karl Elsässer in the observer's pit) engaged three FBA flying boats protected by two single-seat aircraft. The melée ended with Meyer and Elsässer bringing down FBA Serial No 332, code D11. Its crewmen, Enseigne de Vaisseau Robert Guyon d'Asnière de Salins and Sgt Médeville of CAM Dunkirk, were brought to Zeebrugge as prisoners of war.

With that success, Meyer became the *Kriegsmarine's* first pilot

Zeebrugge's first high-scoring pilot, Flgmt Karl Meyer distinguished himself in an interesting variety of seaplanes before moving on to conventional land-based fighters (*Private collection of Milosz Zielinski*)

A captured FBA Type H flying boat of CAM Dunkirk is brought into Zeebrugge. FBAs were twice brought down by the two-seater team of Karl Meyer and Erich Bönisch (*Private collection of Milosz Zielinski*)

Flgobmt Meyer and mascot pose before his favourite seaplane, the single-seat Rumpler 6B 1 Nr 788. Although it was intrinsically at a disadvantage against land-based fighters, Meyer used it to bring down a Sopwith Pup on 1 February 1917 (*Private collection of Milosz Zielinski*)

to make ace, but he was subsequently reminded that he was not invincible when FF 33H Nr 820 developed engine trouble during combat on 1 November. The seaplane crashed offshore but Meyer and Elsässer were rescued uninjured.

Meyer was flying the third prototype Rumpler 6B 1, Nr 788, alongside Niemeyer in Nr 751 as escorts for a pair of two-seat seaplanes when they encountered two Sopwith Pups on 1 February 1917. In spite of the British land fighters' inherent advantages in a dogfight, Meyer managed to force one down on the beach at Breedene. Niemeyer's fight with the second Sopwith ended inconclusively. Meyer's Pup, N6161, was captured intact and restored to airworthiness for evaluation. Its unfortunate pilot, Flt Sub-Lt G L Elliott, had joined the newly formed 3 Naval Squadron just a week earlier.

Obflgmstr Erich Kästner was Flgobmt Meyer's observer when he encountered the British Coastal Airship *C17*, which had been blown far from its regular patrolling station, on 21 April 1916 (*Private collection of Milosz Zielinski*)

Promoted to Flugmeister, Meyer was patrolling with Oberflugmt Erich Kästner as his observer on 21 April when they sighted an airship near Nieuport and gave chase. The Germans held their fire until the range closed to 200 metres, at which point they opened up and the gasbag burst into flames. The British Coastal class airship *C17*, which adverse winds had blown far from its regular station, fell 500 metres into the sea a few miles east of the North Foreland, killing Sub-Lt Edward G O Jackson and Assistant Paymaster R A P Walter.

While Meyer and Bönisch were having their run of successes, Christiansen had also seen his share of clashes with the RNAS. Indeed, he had claimed four victories by 25 April 1917. These apparently failed to meet the official confirmation criteria but that situation was about to change.

At 0600 hrs on 15 May Christiansen, with Ltn z S Hillger as his observer, took off in FF 33L

This postcard shows Meyer and Kästner attacking *C17*. The Germans held their fire until the range had closed to 200 metres, and were within 20 metres when the gasbag burst into flames and fell 500 metres into the sea a few miles east of the North Foreland, killing Sub-Lt Edward G O Jackson and Assistant Paymaster R A P Walter (*Private collection of Milosz Zielinski*)

After several adventures and several unconfirmed victories with SFI 1, Ltn z S Friedrich Christiansen was credited with a 'Sopwith Pup' on 15 May 1917. Second Maître Bernard Vigneau of the CAM was killed in Sopwith 1½ Strutter SH1, code D 21, shortly after he had himself been credited with downing a 'scout' (*HAC/UTD via Greg VanWyngarden*)

Friedrichshafen FF 33L Nr 936, here seen with major float damage, was flown by Flgmstrs Huthmacher and Maukisch on 15 May when they and Ltn z S Röver and Flgmstr Elsässer, in Nr 937, jointly brought down two FBAs. Christiansen and Ltn z S Hillger in Nr 938 were credited with destroying an accompanying Sopwith 1½ Strutter (*Greg VanWyngarden*)

Nr 938, leading Nrs 937 and 936 on an offensive patrol toward the mouth of the Thames. Off the Flemish coast by 0645 hrs, they encountered two FBAs escorted by a Sopwith and immediately attacked. During the course of the fight Christiansen and Hillger sent the Sopwith down vertically to crash into the sea off Dover, while damaged FBAs D 5 and D 12 were forced to land – as was FF 33L Nr 937 with engine trouble. Christiansen landed alongside Nr 937, rescued crewmen Ltn z S d R M A Röver and Flugmt Elsässer and destroyed the crippled floatplane with machine gun fire prior to flying back to Zeebrugge. Meanwhile, FF 33L Nr 936 reported the downed FBAs' location to a German destroyer, which found the flying boats and took their crews prisoner. The Sopwith was confirmed as Christiansen's first undisputed victory.

Christiansen was patrolling with Vzflgmstr Maukisch on 5 June when they spotted German sailors in the water who turned out to be from the destroyer *S20*, which had been sunk in an uneven encounter by the British light cruiser HMS *Conquest*. Landing, Christiansen jettisoned his guns, ammunition and 100 litres of fuel in order to take three survivors aboard. As he laboured to restart a troublesome engine, a further 20 destroyermen swam up, begging to be rescued. 'Only with great violence were these poor people shaken off, to be sentenced to death', Christiansen subsequently wrote. 'It was a difficult decision, but it had to be!'

FBA 409 D 5 sits on the dock at Zeebrugge after it and its crew, Quartier-Maître Antoine Chauvignat and Matelot Philibert, were captured on 15 May. FBA 422 D 12 was also recovered, with Quartier-Maître Boucand and Enseigne de Vaisseau François Carle becoming PoWs too (*Collection of Milosz Zielinski*)

After finally starting his engine, Christiansen took off amid cries of 'You flying dogs won't take us with you! You'll let us drown here wretchedly!' After flying his three charges to Zeebrugge, however, he promptly led 12 seaplanes and four torpedo boats back to the scene, where they rescued 25 seamen and recovered 38 bodies from the North Sea. Although he received the *Rettungsmedaille*, Christiansen commented, 'We participants were affected by this horrific experience for a long time afterwards'.

On 20 June Karl Meyer transferred to *Marine Feld Jasta* (MFJ) I, with which unit he flew an Albatros D V to score his eighth victory – a DH 4 of No 57 Sqn – two days later. The pilot of the aeroplane, Lt P H Bigwood, was killed. Meyer rejoined SFl I on 11 September, but on 16 October he helped organise the first *Seefrontstaffel*, which was to bolster the local defences with single-seat fighters. Karl Meyer's distinguished naval career abruptly ended in Leipzig on 31 December 1917 when he died of injuries following a flying accident three days earlier.

On 15 September 1917 Kaptlt z S Tschirschky was appointed *Gruppenkommandeur der Seeflieger* and Christiansen, promoted to Oberleutnant zur See, succeeded him in command of SFl I. By that time the unit was receiving a new, compact, robust two-seat seaplane in the form of the Brandenburg W 12.

Designed by Ernst Heinkel, who as an employee of the Hansa-Brandenburg Werke had created a number of naval aircraft for both Austria-Hungary and Germany, the W 12 had a conventional biplane structure but featured a rudder that extended below rather than above the fuselage in order to give the observer a less obstructed field of fire. Powered by a 160 hp Mercedes D III or 150 hp Benz Bz III engine and armed with one or two synchronised LMG 08/15 machine guns forward and a flexible Parabellum gun aft, the W 12 entered service in 1917. Some 146 were built, to which the Dutch, after interning one, obtained a licence to build a further 35. The W 12's 100 mph speed and three-and-a-half-hour endurance made it well suited to patrolling the North Sea.

On 1 October Christiansen, in W 12 Nr 1183, with Ltn z S Hillger as his observer, graphically demonstrated the new seaplane's capabilities when he drove a Felixstowe-based Porte FB 2 Baby flying boat down off Texel with bullets in its left engine and radiator. This was confirmed as his second victory, despite the fact that its crew, Flt Cdr N S Douglas and Flt Lt B D Hobbs, managed to taxi their mount back to England.

On 11 December Christiansen, again in Nr 1183, with Flgmt Bernhard Wladicka as his observer, was leading a three-seaplane patrol when he encountered Astra-Torres airship *C27* near the Nord Hinder lightship at 1010 hrs. Giving chase, Christiansen caught up with the airship at 1030 hrs and attacked at an altitude of 400 metres, shooting

Christiansen's Hansa-Brandenburg W 12 Nr 1183 (bottom right) is seen at Zeebrugge. Distinguished by a rudder that extended below the fuselage to provide the observer with a clearer field of fire, the robust W 12 had a 100 mph maximum speed and three-and-a-half-hour endurance (*via Harry Dempsey*)

it down in flames at 1032 hrs. *C27's* crew, Flt Lts John F Dixon DFC and Herbert Fail, AM2 John C Collett and AM1s James E Martin and Ernest R White, were killed. On the same day that he destroyed *C27*, Christiansen received the *Orden Pour le Mérite* for the 440 operational flights he had completed by then.

Oblt z S Friedrich Christiansen was leading a three-seaplane patrol of Hansa-Brandenburg W 12s from Zeebrugge naval station on 15 February 1918 when, at 1045 hrs, they sighted an Allied convoy being escorted by two Felixstowe-based Curtiss H-12B Large America flying boats. The latter both fled, but upon being overtaken at 1100 hrs, one of them made a fight of it until shot down in flames from an altitude of 200 metres near Nord Hinder lightship. Heavy seas prevented the Germans from landing near the wreckage, which turned out to be H-12B N4338. The flying boat's crew, Canadian Flt Lt Claude C Purdy, Ens Albert D Sturtevant, Boy Mech Arthur Hector Stephenson and AM1 Sidney James Hollidge, perished. Christiansen and his observer shared the victory with Flgobermt Urban and Ltn z S Ehrhard.

Albert Dillon Sturtevant, an officer of the US Naval Reserve (USNR), was among the 29 members of the First Yale Unit that had been attached to RNAS Felixstowe since October 1917. The first American of any military branch to die in aerial combat in his own country's service during World War 1, Sturtevant was posthumously awarded the Navy Cross. A destroyer was later named for him.

On 23 April the Royal Navy mounted a daring raid on Zeebrugge, intending to sink three old cruisers loaded with concrete within the port so as to block passage to U-boats and light vessels, while the explosives-packed submarine *C3* was blown up to destroy the viaduct connecting the mile-long mole to the shore. Although 200 British sailors were killed and 300 wounded, and eight Victoria Crosses awarded among the participants, the raid was only partially successful. Within two days of the attack the Germans had cleared a passage for U-boats to transit Zeebrugge into the Channel.

The next day (24 April) Christiansen shot down a Felixstowe-based Curtiss H-8 flying boat off Nord Hinder lightship. Then, on the 25th, while leading a five-seaplane patrol, he sighted two Felixstowe-based flying boats that fled to the northeast until the

A postcard of the attack by Christiansen and his observer, Flgmt Bernhard Wladicka, on British Astra-Torres airship *C27* near the Nord Hinder lightship on 11 December 1917 (*Greg VanWyngarden*)

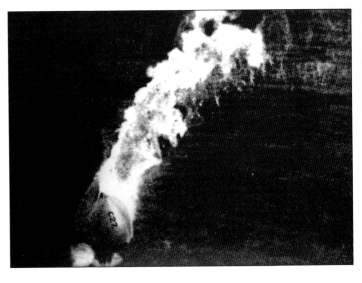

A photograph, evidently retouched, purporting to show *C27* descending in flames after Christiansen's attack. In direct consequence of this incident the Royal Navy prohibited airship patrols within range of German aeroplanes along the Flanders coast (*Colin Owers*)

Germans overtook one of them. Christiansen closed to within ten metres of his quarry and Wladicka fired a 100-round broadside into the port engine, which burst into flames. H-12B No 8677 fell into the sea near Outer Gabbard three minutes later, killing Capt N A Magor and Ens Stephen Potter USNR. The first US Navy pilot to be credited with downing an enemy aeroplane, 22-year-old Potter, like Sturtevant, subsequently had a destroyer named in his honour. The only German casualty was Flgmt Neubert, who suffered minor wounds.

April saw the first deliveries of a new seaplane scout in the form of the Brandenburg W 29. In early 1918 Christiansen had told Ernst Heinkel that a more up-to-date successor to the W 12 would be needed if his station was to maintain its edge over the North Sea. Heinkel's response

Curtiss H-12B No 8677 at Felixstowe before it was shot down by Zeebrugge-based W 12s off Nord Hinder lightship on 25 April 1918, its destruction being credited to Christiansen and Wladicka. Although the crew perished, they were credited with downing one of their attackers moments prior to their demise. This made Ens Stephen Potter the first US Navy airman to achieve an aerial victory. In reality, the only German casualty was Flgmt Neubert, who was wounded by return fire from the H-12B (*Imperial War Museum MH 2864*)

A Felixstowe F 2A burns after being strafed by Christiansen and his flight. This may be F 2A N5433, which had force landed and was taxiing homeward off Terschelling on 4 June 1918 when Christiansen and his W 29s caught it and claimed the flying boat as a victory (*Colin Owers*)

Christiansen leads a typical five-seaplane wedge formation on patrol over the North Sea. When under attack by Allied fighters, the W 29s adopted a stepped wedge formation for enhanced defence (*Colin Owers*)

was to produce a monoplane version of the W 12, with span and chord increased to approximate the biplane's overall wing area, braced by struts emanating from the floats. The seaplane could achieve a speed of 109.375 mph and had an endurance of four hours. Armament on 38 of the 78 W 29s produced consisted of two machine guns forward and one aft, while the remaining 40 seaplanes carried radio equipment in place of one of the synchronised guns.

Christiansen test flew the W 29 prototype at Brandenburg, and he was so pleased with the seaplane that he insisted upon flying it back to Zeebrugge for operational use without further ado. He was certainly flying one on 4 June when he and his flight caught Felixstowe F 2A N5433 off Terschelling. The flying boat had in fact already force landed in the water and was taxiing to shore when the Germans set it on fire, but it was credited to Christiansen as an aerial victory.

'Opposing enemy seaplane units in our area was comparatively easy to do, as our Hansa-Brandenburg monoplanes were superior to the British flying boats', explained Ltn z S Fritz Stormer, who flew W 29s in Christiansen's 1 *Staffel*. 'On the other hand, the drag of our twin pontoons put us at a serious disadvantage in terms of speed, manoeuvrability and armament if we were ambushed on takeoff or landing by British or French land-based biplane fighters.

'Generally, the *Staffel* flew in a wedge-shaped formation', he continued, 'with the *Staffelkapitän* in the leading seaplane. Behind him and to the right was the W 29 crewed by the photo officer and deputy commander of the unit. During an attack by fighters coming in from above and behind, the seaplanes would descend even lower so that a sloping V was formed and all machine guns had an unobstructed field of fire. This defensive manoeuvre had been learned through hard experience, and it made land-based enemy fighters respect our formations. Gliding along close to the surface of the water gave us a slight advantage when we were subjected to a classic attack from above and behind.

'The comradeship among the crews – officers and enlisted men alike – was splendid! Each would have sacrificed himself for the other. Among the officer corps at the seaplane station, this feeling was of course advanced by Christiansen's superior qualities as a leader.'

Christensen, in his W 29, scored a double victory southeast of Nord Hinder lightship on 4 July, while a third 'Englander' was brought down by one of his three wingmen. As had been the case at least once before,

Two Hansa-Brandenburg W 29s take off on patrol from Zeebrugge. Oblt z S Christiansen's Nr 2512, bearing his black 'C' monogram in a diamond within a white diagonal band, can be seen in the background (*Colin Owers*)

On 6 July 1918 Christiansen's 1 *Staffel* caught submarine *C25* surfacing in the Thames Estuary. After firing 5000 rounds at it in 35 minutes, the Germans contacted Zeebrugge by wireless and brought in more seaplanes from 2 *Staffel*, led by Ltn z S Philipp Becht. A German observer photographed the submarine's ordeal (*Colin Owers*)

however, the results were not as decisive as they seemed. Felixstowe-based F 2As 4297 and 4513 were forced down, with Engineer Hopely dead and three crewmen wounded, but they were later recovered, while the damaged F 2A 4540 likewise managed to return home when its engineer, AM2 Blacklock, stepped out on the starboard wing while under attack and stopped an oil leak in the engine with his hand. All three flying boats later returned to operations.

'It was almost routine with us that whenever "Krischan" took off, something would happen', recalled Stormer. A case in point occurred on 6 July when Christiansen, leading four other W 29s, caught submarine *C25* surfacing in the Thames Estuary. After a 35-minute strafing attack, in which they expended 5000 rounds, the seaplanes sent a wireless message to Zeebrugge, which summoned floatplanes of 2 *Staffel*, led by Ltn z S Philipp Becht. 'They found the British submarine being towed by a sister boat, *E51*', Stormer reported. 'As soon as the leading submarine spotted the second wave of our aircraft the towline was immediately severed and the undamaged submarine made a crash dive beneath the water'.

Becht's flight spotted the damaged *C25* under tow by *E51*, at which point the latter vessel severed the towline and submerged. Again left to defend itself with its own crew-served machine guns, *C25* came under more gunfire and was also attacked with 5- and 10-kg bombs (*Colin Owers*)

A W 29 overflies *C25* after making a strafing pass. The Germans killed the vessel's skipper, Lt David C Bell, and five crewmen in the attack, but contrary to the credit they all received for its demise, the battered boat made it home (*Colin Owers*)

Becht's crews subjected *C25* to more machine gun fire, as well as 5- and 10-kg bombs, after which Stormer noted, 'We were satisfied that the boat had been put out of action'. In actuality, although the submarine had indeed been damaged and its captain, Lt David C Bell, and five crewmen killed during the course of the attack, *C25* managed to return to port.

Christiansen was leading a six-seaplane patrol of 1 *Staffel* W 29s on 18 July when they encountered Short 184s N2927 and N2937 of the Marine Aeroplane Depot at Westgate, escorted by two Manston-based Sopwith Camels. In spite of the Camels' effort to prevent their attacks, Christiansen and Wladicka and the crew of Ltn z S d R Hahn and Flgmster Hess shared in the destruction of both floatplanes southeast of Kentish Knock, killing all four crewmen. Christiansen's 13th, and final, claim was over Yarmouth-based F 2A N4305, downed off Lowestoft on 31 July.

Christiansen, who had by now attained the rank of Kapitänleutnant, was given command of the II *Seeflugbattalion* on 31 October 1918. In the wake of a war that ended with much of the *Kriegsmarine* in a state of mutiny, he served in the 3rd *Marinebrigade* under Wilfried von Löwenfeld until his formal retirement on 6 March 1919. In 1922 Christiansen returned to sea with the merchant marine, serving as captain of the Hamburg-based steamship *Rio Bravo* from 1924 to 1930. He then joined Dornier, piloting the giant Do X flying boat across the Atlantic in 1930. In 1933 Christiansen became actively involved in Adolf Hitler's government, joining the Aviation Ministry that year and being appointed *Korpsführer* of the newly founded *Nationalsozialistische Flieger Korps*, with the rank of Generalleutnant, on 30 April 1937. He rose to General der Flieger the following year.

During World War 2 Christiansen was made *Wehrmachtsbefehlshaber in der Niederlanden* on 28 March 1940 at Reischmarshall Hermann Göring's recommendation. He also filled the parallel position of Supreme Commander of the 25th Army from 10 November 1944 to 28 January 1945.

Although not the most fanatical of Nazi supporters, Christiansen ordered the shooting of Dutch hostages in August 1942 and subsequently gained his greatest notoriety for the reprisal at Putten. On 30 September 1944 Dutch resistance fighters ambushed a German staff car outside Putten, mortally wounding an officer and capturing a second. Christiansen's response was, 'Put them all against the wall and burn the place down'. On 2 October the SS duly deported all of Putten's male residents aged between 16 and 50 to labour camps. Seven were shot in the roundup and 661 deported, 59 later being sent home and 13 escaping by jumping from the trains. Of the 589 sent to Ladelund concentration camp, only 49 returned alive.

When Allied forces liberated the Netherlands, Christiansen's command ceased on 7 April 1945 and the British arrested him on 5 July. On 12 February 1948 the Dutch convicted him of war crimes and he was sentenced to 12 years imprisonment in Arnhem jail, although he was given a premature Christmas release on 19 December 1951. Returning to West Germany, Christiansen died at Aufkrug on 5 December 1972, a week short of his 93rd birthday.

Zeebrugge personnel recover an RNAS Short 184 brought down in German-controlled waters. Christiansen's penultimate aerial success was to shoot down two Short 184s in spite of the efforts of their Sopwith Camel escorts (*Private collection of Milosz Zielinski*)

Awarded the *Orden Pour le Mérite* and credited with 13 victories (including airship *C27* and submarine *C25*), Christiansen acquired a different sort of notoriety during World War 2. In 1948 the Dutch government sentenced him to 12 years in prison for war crimes in the Netherlands (*Greg VanWyngarden*)

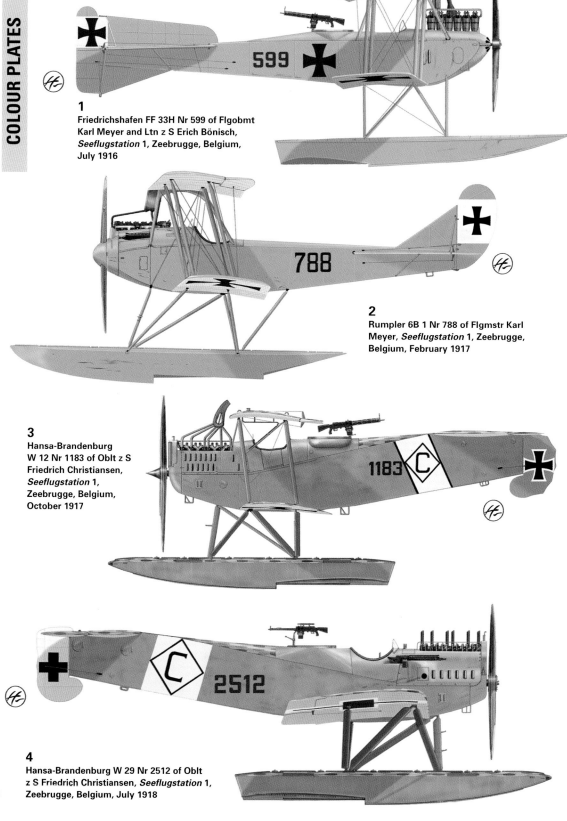

1

Friedrichshafen FF 33H Nr 599 of Flgobmt
Karl Meyer and Ltn z S Erich Bönisch,
Seeflugstation 1, Zeebrugge, Belgium,
July 1916

2

Rumpler 6B 1 Nr 788 of Flgmstr Karl
Meyer, *Seeflugstation* 1, Zeebrugge,
Belgium, February 1917

3

Hansa-Brandenburg
W 12 Nr 1183 of Oblt z S
Friedrich Christiansen,
Seeflugstation 1,
Zeebrugge, Belgium,
October 1917

4

Hansa-Brandenburg W 29 Nr 2512 of Oblt
z S Friedrich Christiansen, *Seeflugstation* 1,
Zeebrugge, Belgium, July 1918

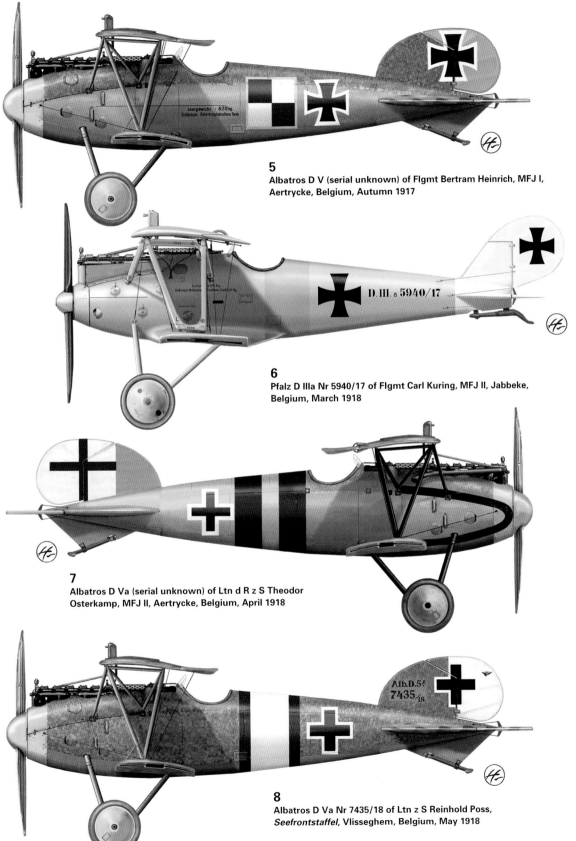

5
Albatros D V (serial unknown) of Flgmt Bertram Heinrich, MFJ I,
Aertrycke, Belgium, Autumn 1917

6
Pfalz D IIIa Nr 5940/17 of Flgmt Carl Kuring, MFJ II, Jabbeke,
Belgium, March 1918

7
Albatros D Va (serial unknown) of Ltn d R z S Theodor
Osterkamp, MFJ II, Aertrycke, Belgium, April 1918

8
Albatros D Va Nr 7435/18 of Ltn z S Reinhold Poss,
Seefrontstaffel, Vlisseghem, Belgium, May 1918

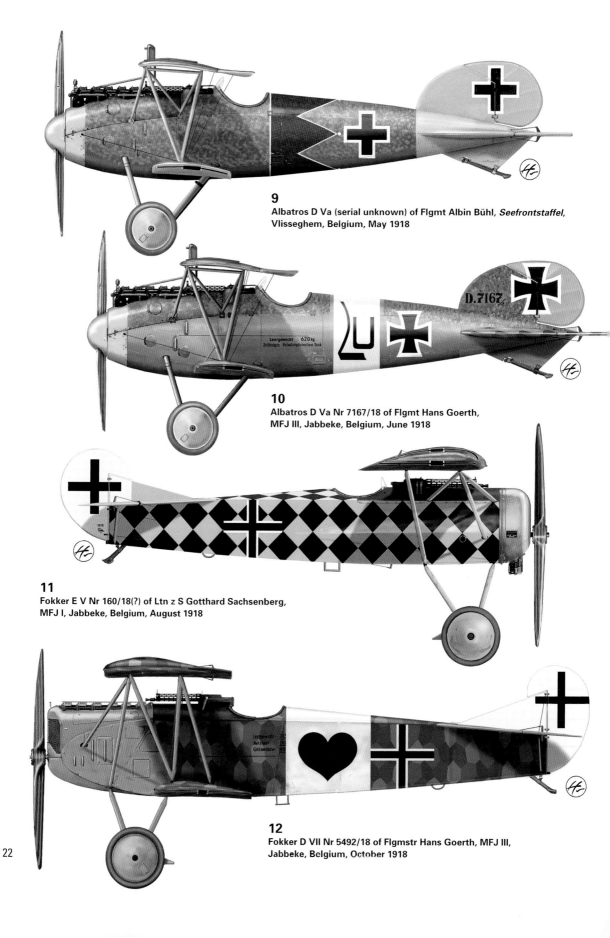

9
Albatros D Va (serial unknown) of Flgmt Albin Bühl, *Seefrontstaffel*,
Vlisseghem, Belgium, May 1918

10
Albatros D Va Nr 7167/18 of Flgmt Hans Goerth,
MFJ III, Jabbeke, Belgium, June 1918

11
Fokker E V Nr 160/18(?) of Ltn z S Gotthard Sachsenberg,
MFJ I, Jabbeke, Belgium, August 1918

12
Fokker D VII Nr 5492/18 of Flgmstr Hans Goerth, MFJ III,
Jabbeke, Belgium, October 1918

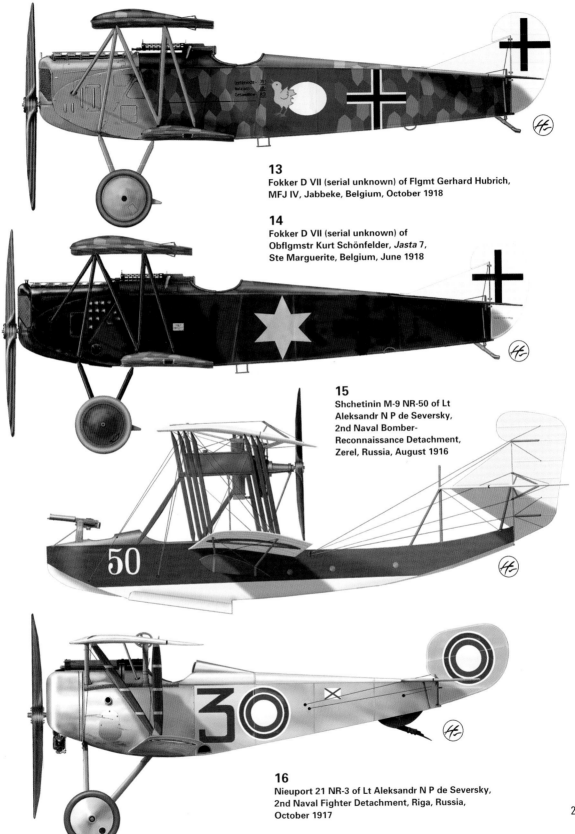

13
Fokker D VII (serial unknown) of Flgmt Gerhard Hubrich,
MFJ IV, Jabbeke, Belgium, October 1918

14
Fokker D VII (serial unknown) of
Obflgmstr Kurt Schönfelder, *Jasta* 7,
Ste Marguerite, Belgium, June 1918

15
Shchetinin M-9 NR-50 of Lt
Aleksandr N P de Seversky,
2nd Naval Bomber-
Reconnaissance Detachment,
Zerel, Russia, August 1916

16
Nieuport 21 NR-3 of Lt Aleksandr N P de Seversky,
2nd Naval Fighter Detachment, Riga, Russia,
October 1917

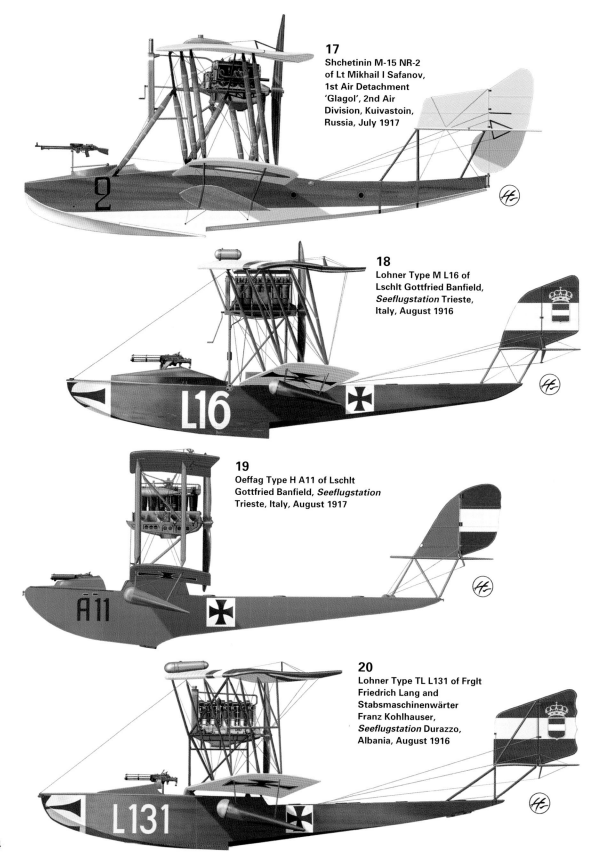

17
Shchetinin M-15 NR-2
of Lt Mikhail I Safanov,
1st Air Detachment
'Glagol', 2nd Air
Division, Kuivastoin,
Russia, July 1917

18
Lohner Type M L16 of
Lschlt Gottfried Banfield,
Seeflugstation Trieste,
Italy, August 1916

19
Oeffag Type H A11 of Lschlt
Gottfried Banfield, *Seeflugstation*
Trieste, Italy, August 1917

20
Lohner Type TL L131 of Frglt
Friedrich Lang and
Stabsmaschinenwärter
Franz Kohlhauser,
Seeflugstation Durazzo,
Albania, August 1916

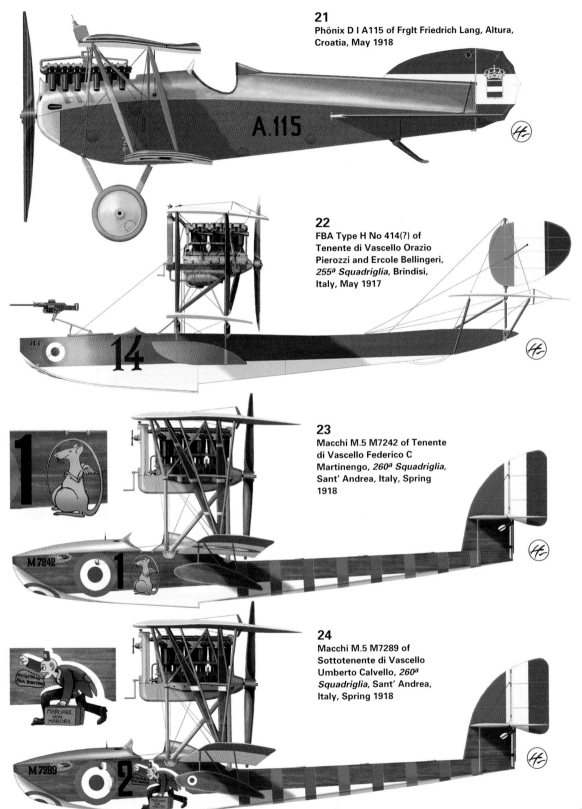

21
Phönix D I A115 of Frglt Friedrich Lang, Altura, Croatia, May 1918

22
FBA Type H No 414(?) of Tenente di Vascello Orazio Pierozzi and Ercole Bellingeri, *255ª Squadriglia*, Brindisi, Italy, May 1917

23
Macchi M.5 M7242 of Tenente di Vascello Federico C Martinengo, *260ª Squadriglia*, Sant' Andrea, Italy, Spring 1918

24
Macchi M.5 M7289 of Sottotenente di Vascello Umberto Calvello, *260ª Squadriglia*, Sant' Andrea, Italy, Spring 1918

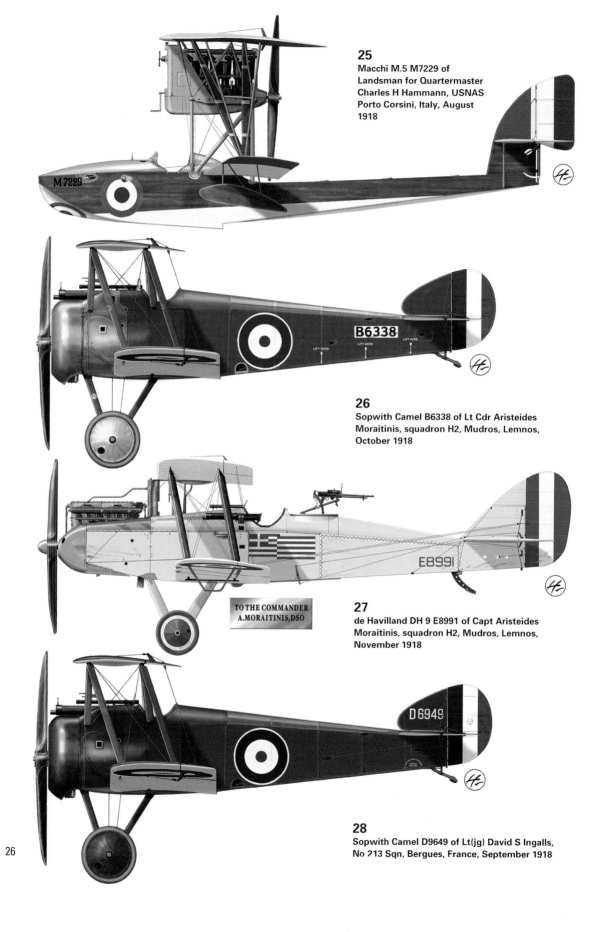

25
Macchi M.5 M7229 of
Landsman for Quartermaster
Charles H Hammann, USNAS
Porto Corsini, Italy, August
1918

26
Sopwith Camel B6338 of Lt Cdr Aristeides
Moraitinis, squadron H2, Mudros, Lemnos,
October 1918

TO THE COMMANDER
A.MORAITINIS,DSO

27
de Havilland DH 9 E8991 of Capt Aristeides
Moraitinis, squadron H2, Mudros, Lemnos,
November 1918

28
Sopwith Camel D9649 of Lt(jg) David S Ingalls,
No 213 Sqn, Bergues, France, September 1918

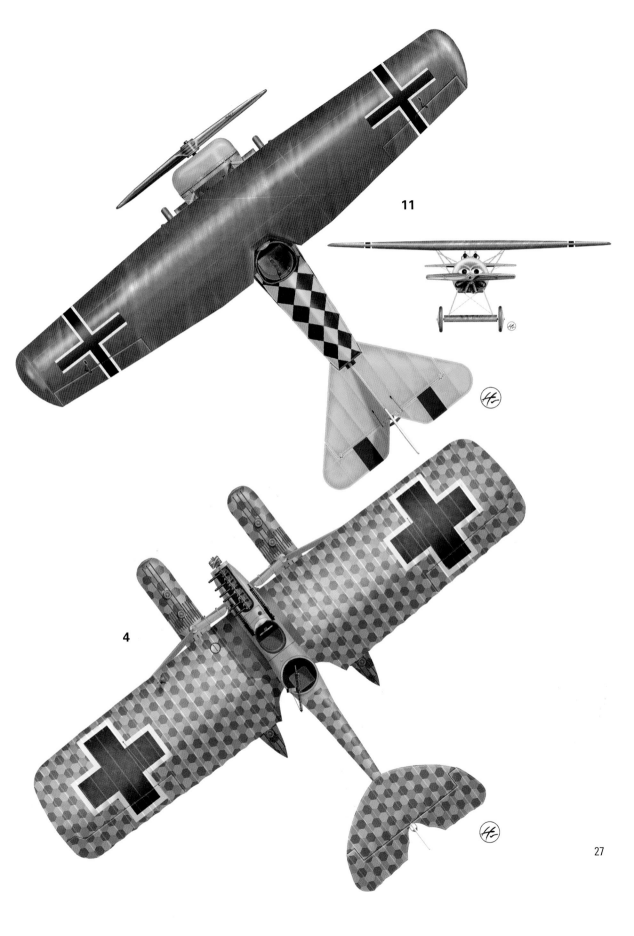

11

4

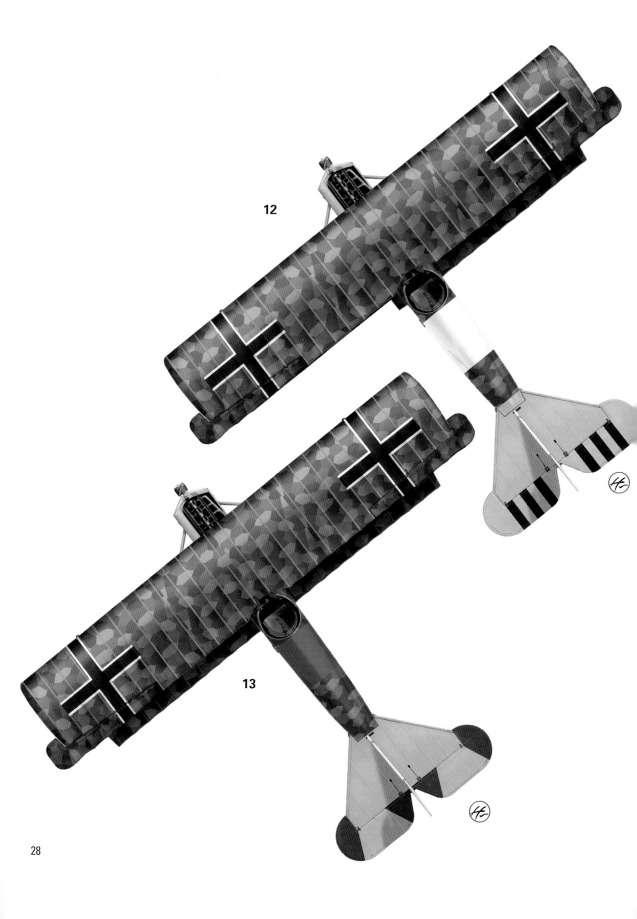

12

13

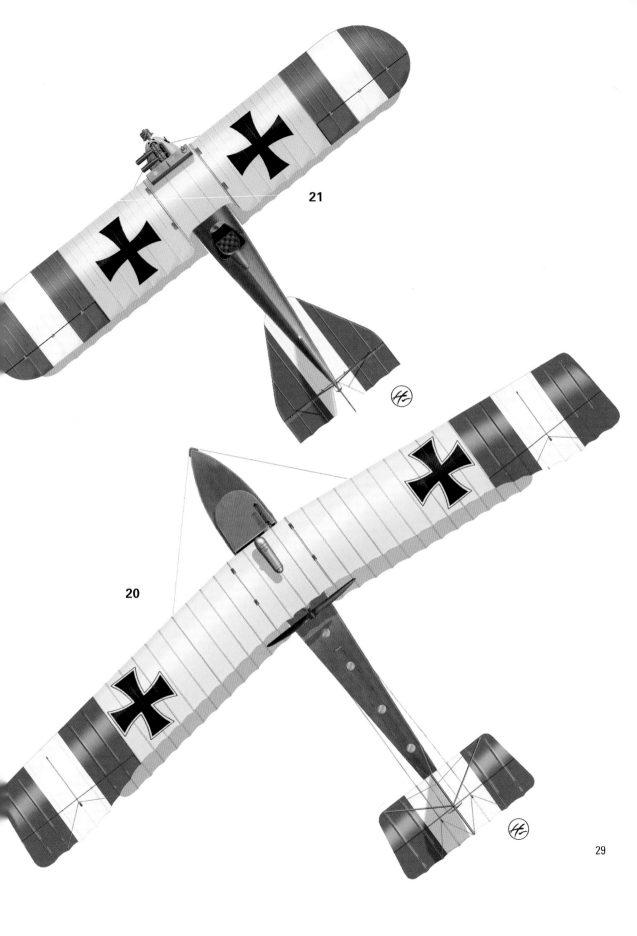

21

20

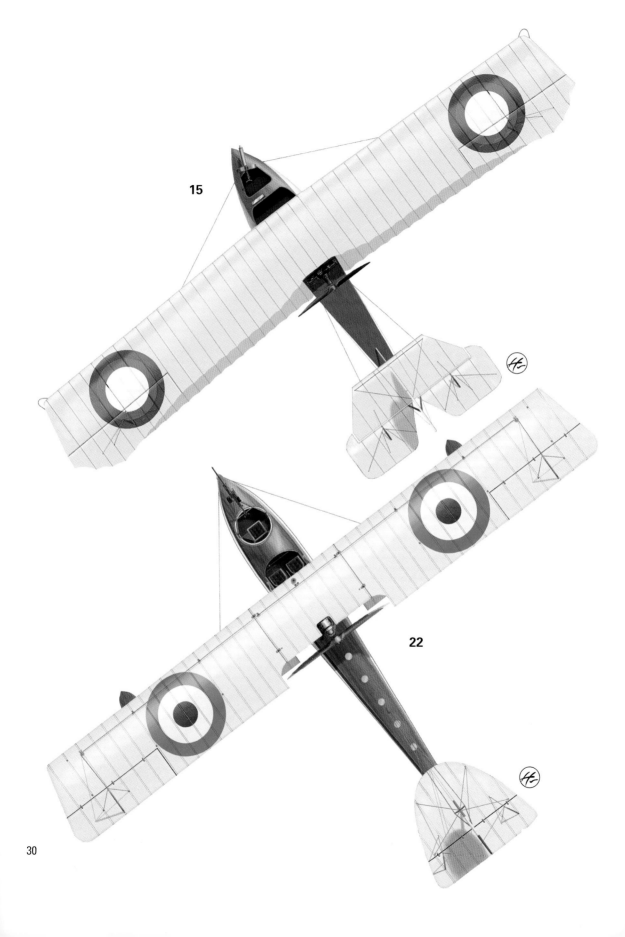

15

22

THE MARINE FELD JASTAS

Although the Germans boasted some formidable two-seat seaplanes, the evolution of the single-seat land-based fighter in 1915 made it necessary for the *Kriegsmarine* to counter the threat with single-seaters of its own. This included some seaplane types such as the Rumpler 6B 1, Brandenburg KDW and CC and Albatros W 4, as well as a number of experimental types. The KDW (for *Kampf Doppeldecker Wasser*, or waterborne battle biplane) was a seaplane version of the Austro-Hungarian Brandenburg D I 'star-strutter', of which 58 were supplied to the German navy. The Albatros W 4, which entered service in September 1916, was an enlarged version of the Albatros D II on floats, and 118 had been built by December 1917.

The Germans also purchased 26 Brandenburg CC single-seat flying boats, using 150 hp Benz Bz IIIs in place of the Austrian version's Austro-Daimler or Hiero engines. In spite of a commendable top speed of 109.373 mph (175 km/h), they saw little use mainly because of a German preference for seaplanes rather than flying boats. In any case, even the single-seaters ended up being eclipsed by the outstanding two-seat Brandenburg W 12 and W 29.

To counter the threat posed by Allied single-seat biplane scouts that were now prowling the Flanders coast in ever growing numbers, the

Ltn z S Gotthard Sachsenberg stands at right beside an LVG C II of MFFA I early in 1916. He soon departed for fighter training, with the aim of providing these two-seaters with a single-seat escort (*HAC/UTD via Greg VanWyngarden*)

Kriegsmarine was ultimately compelled to acquire land-based fighters from the *Luftstreiskräfte* to equip its own *Marine Feld Jagdstaffeln* (MFJ). The first such unit – MFJ I – was formed at Neumünster, in the German 4. *Armee* sector, on 1 February 1917 under the command of Ltn z S Gotthard Sachsenberg.

Born in Rosslau, near Dessau, on 6 December 1891, Gotthard Sachsenberg grew up in the same town and went to the same school as Germany's innovative 40-victory ace Oswald Boelcke. He became a sea cadet in 1913, but when war broke out in 1914 he joined the *Freiwillige Marineflugkorps* and was assigned as an observer with *Marine Feldflieger Abteilung* (MFFA) II on 22 February 1915. In that capacity, Sachsenberg served commendably enough to receive the Iron Cross 1st Class, and was promoted from fähnrich zur see to leutnant zur see in early 1916.

While serving as an instructor for observers, Saschsenberg requested flight training and was sent to learn to fly fighters at Mannheim. In April 1916 he led a *Kampf Einsitzer Kommando* (KEK) attached to MFFA I, flying Fokker E IIIs from Mariakerke. At that time another KEK was providing fighter backup to MFFA II at Neumünster, and on 1 February 1917 both units were combined to form the first *Marine Feld Jasta*.

Initially equipped with Albatros D IIIs, MFJ I logged its first victory on 7 February when Vzflgmstr Josef Wirtz shot down Sopwith 1½ Strutter N5102 of 5 Naval Wing RNAS, killing Flt Lt C R Blagrove and 2AM Milne. On 15 April the *Jasta* moved to Aertrycke, southeast of Ostende. The unit's next successes came nine days later in the form of two FE 2ds credited posthumously to Wirtz, who reportedly fell to his death over Becelaere in Albatros D III 2281/16 after colliding with his last victim. The only FE unit active in the Ypres sector that day was No 20 Sqn, which was also set upon by *Jasta* 8, from which Offstv Walter Göttsch and Ltn Werner Junck claimed an FE apiece, and *Jasta* 18, whose Ltn Walter von Bülow-Bothkamp also claimed an FE.

There seems to have been some multiple claiming in the melée, because No 20 Sqn's losses amounted to FE 2d A6385, in which 2Lt A R Johnson and Lt H R Nicholson were killed, A6403, brought down safely in Allied

Sachsenberg sits in the rightmost chair beside a Fokker E III of the KEK he led at Mariakerke from April 1916 in support of MFFA I. On 1 February 1917 this unit and the KEK for MFFA II were combined to form the first *Marine Feld Jagdstaffel* (Greg VanWyngarden)

Ltn z S Wilhelm Mattheus and Ltn d R z S Theodor Osterkamp (holding his camera) pose with their groundcrew before LVG C II LF 1436 of MFFA I, in which they claimed a Farman shot down on 6 September 1916. This success was not confirmed, however (*Greg VanWyngarden*)

lines by 2Lt E O Perry and 2AM Edward H Sayers, and A5144, which was set alight but whose wounded pilot, Lt N L Robertson, managed to make the Allied side before crashing. He was pulled from the burning wreck by his wounded observer, Capt R M Knowles. The 'Fee' crews in turn claimed five German aircraft destroyed, including one to Perry and Sayers – the latter's second of an eventual five victories. In addition to MFJ I's loss of Wirtz, *Jasta* 18's Ltn Fritz Kleindienst jumped from his burning Albatros and the unit's *Staffelführer*, Rittm Karl von Grieffenhagen, was wounded in the leg and lower jaw.

MFJ I's fourth victory was also the first for the *Kriegsmarine's* future 'ace of aces', Ltn d R z S Theodor Osterkamp, who downed a Nieuport 23 near Oostkerke on 30 April. Its pilot, Adj Baron Maurice E A M Siraut of the *9éme Escadrille Belge*, force landed in Allied lines unhurt.

'Theo' Osterkamp was born in Aschersleben, in the Rhineland, on 15 April 1892, and was studying forestry when war broke out. Turned down by the German army because of his slight build, he enlisted in the *Freiwillige Marineflugkorps* in August 1914 and spent the next two years as an observer with *Marine Flieger Abteilungen* on the Belgian coast. Osterkamp usually flew with Ltn z S Wilhelm Mattheus, and he scored his first, albeit unconfirmed, victory with him. Commissioned in July 1916, Osterkamp underwent pilot training in March 1917 and was posted to MFJ I on 14 April.

Sachsenberg finally opened his account in high style on 1 May when he downed a Farman and a Sopwith 1½ Strutter over Dixmude. A second 1½ Strutter was credited to MFJ I as being brought down west of Dixmude by Flgmt Bertram Heinrich – another early enlistee in the naval air arm, he had been born in Chartlottenberg on 29 March

1894. One, or perhaps even both, of the Sopwiths was probably an elusively handled machine of the *6éme Escadrille Belge* whose pilot managed to shake off his four attackers. Upon landing, he counted 32 bullet holes in his aeroplane, 29 of them without leaving the cockpit! In spite of his Sopwith being badly shot up, future Belgian 'ace of aces' 1Sgt Willy Coppens, and his observer Capt Gustave Declercq, survived unhurt.

The only confirmed Belgian loss on 1 May was a Farman F 40 of the *3éme Escadrille Belge* in which Sgt Jean Pauli and Lt Jean de Bersaques were killed. Clouding the matter further is the fact that Ltn Karl-Emil Schäfter, commander of *Jasta* 28, claimed a Farman in the same location that afternoon.

On 12 May Royal Navy vessels bombarded Zeebrugge, covered by Pups of 4 Naval Squadron and Triplanes of 'Naval 10'. MFJ I had several engagements with the British fighters, during which Sachsenberg was credited with a Sopwith off Zeebrugge, Heinrich claimed a second northwest of the port and Osterkamp a third off Ostende. 'Naval 4' claimed three German fighters and two seaplanes for the loss of a scout in the Zeebrugge area. Osterkamp's quarry may have been Flt Sub-Lt Raymond Collishaw, who was driven off a seaplane that he was attacking near Ostende by two fighters, but returned unscathed.

On 25 May Heinrich forced Short 184 No 6090 to land in the North Sea off Westende, its crew, from the Dunkirk Seaplane Station, being picked up by a U-boat. On 3 June Heinrich and Flgmt Künstler were each credited with a Nieuport downed north of Ypres. Two days later a patrol of MFJ I fighters was waiting to rendezvous with 22 Gotha bombers returning from a raid on Sheerness when it encountered five Triplanes and two Pups of 'Naval 9' off Ostende. The ensuing scrap resulted in a Triplane credited to Osterkamp, while Flt Sub-Lts Oliver Le Boutillier, John C Tanner and John W Pinder were each credited with an Albatros out of control. Curiously, no casualties were recorded on either side.

On 7 June the British launched their offensive at Messines, and Sachsenberg marked the occasion with a double victory – an FE 2d downed near Mont St Eloi, killing 2Lt B S Marshall and Pte C Lloyd of No 20 Sqn, and a 'Naval 3' Pup near Potyze, as well as an unconfirmed Sopwith. That same day Flgmstr Ottomar Haggenmüller downed Nieuport B1674 near Bixschoote, Lt J W Shaw of No 40 Sqn RFC becoming a PoW, and Flgmt Künstler claimed another Nieuport, but Flgmt Fritz Kühn was shot down – possibly by Flt Sub-Lt John E Sharman of 'Naval 10' – and taken prisoner, later dying of his wounds at Staden.

On 8 June Vzflgmstr H Bottler downed Triplane N5491 of 'Naval 1' north of Warneton, killing New Zealander Flt Lt Thomas G Culling, who was a six-victory ace. MFJ I had the worst of a dogfight with Belgian Nieuports on the 14th, however, with Vzflgmstr Kurt Lichtherz being killed over Middelkerke, probably by Adj Edmond Thieffry of the *5éme Escadrille Belge*, and Bottler force landing near Ghistelles with wounds to his arm and hand.

On 3 July Thieffry became the first Belgian to be credited with a double victory when he ambushed a flight of MFJ I Albatros D IIIs

Rejected by the German army for being too puny to be a soldier, Theodor Osterkamp joined the navy and went on to become its leading ace. His first confirmed success, near Oostkerke on 30 April 1917, was over a Nieuport 23 whose Belgian pilot, Adj Baron Maurice E A M Siraut of the *5éme Escadrille Belge*, force landed unhurt in Allied lines (*Greg VanWyngarden*)

and shot down two in as many minutes. One of the pilots, Ltn z S Kurt Krüger, was wounded. On 6 July Heinrich downed Triplane N5435 of 'Naval 1' at Reckem, killing Flt Sub-Lt E C Hillaby. Osterkamp scored next, claiming a 1½ Strutter on 11 July.

With the British shifting their offensive focus north to Flanders, MFJ I began seeing more action, sometimes alongside such elite units as Rittm Manfred *Freiherr* von Richthofen's *Jagdgeschwader* I, comprised of *Jastas* 4, 6, 10 and 11. This seems to have been the case on 12 July, when *Jastas* 4 and 36 and MFJ I encountered SE 5s of No 56 Sqn, Pups of No 66 Sqn and some Nieuports and SPADs over Zandvoorde at 2100 hrs. An estimated 60 aeroplanes took part in the sprawling dogfight that ensued.

Among the five SEs of 'Fighting 56', 2Lt Robert G Jardine was attacked by at least two enemy scouts, which he eluded by going into an inverted spin. As he came out of it he almost collided with another German fighter, stalled under a third and fired on it, then came head-on at a fourth, firing 20 rounds before he saw it spin away. Capt Richard A Maybery had to break off at least one attack when enemy fighters attacked him. Although both pilots returned unscathed, as did all of No 66 Sqn's Pups, *Jasta* 4's Vfw Otto Marquardt was credited with an SE 5 destroyed and MFJ I's Osterkamp with either a Sopwith or an SE 5 victory, while Ltn Heinrich Bongartz of *Jasta* 36 was credited with a Sopwith and Ltn Alfred Hubner of *Jasta* 4 with a Triplane. On the British side, No 56 Sqn claimed four victories and No 66 Sqn two. The only German casualties were from *Jasta* 36, whose Vfw Maier was wounded and Ltn Edwin Kreutzer forced to crash land unhurt in friendly territory.

After an unconfirmed Camel claim on 26 July, Heinrich scored his sixth victory on the 27th when he killed Flt Sub-Lt E J K Buckley of 'Naval 4' in Pup N6174 west of Nieuwpoort. MFJ I, however, lost Vzflgmstr Otto Brandt, shot down in flames between Middelkerke and Westende probably by Canadian Flt Sub-Lt James H Forman of 'Naval 6' in Camel N6358 for his second of an eventual nine victories.

Sachsenberg was credited with a SPAD VII northeast of Lampernisse on 9 August, although it may have been a misidentified SE 5 of No 56 Sqn, whose pilot, 2Lt Gordon Ross-Soden, was wounded in the knee. He managed to disengage from combat following Lt Leonard M Barlow's intervention, subsequently making it home. Now with six victories to his name, Sachsenberg was awarded the Knight's Cross with Swords of the Hohenzollern House Order on 20 August. The month was somewhat soured, however, by the death of Flgobmt Luitjen Luitjens over Beerst

MFJ I Albatros scouts line up at Aertrycke in the late summer of 1917. The fifth aeroplane from the left may bear the black and yellow bands of Ltn z S Theo Osterkamp, while the sixth features the ornate band of Ltn z S Friedrich von Götz, who was killed on 11 September 1917. The eighth, adorned with a swastika, was flown by Vzflgmstr Hechner, the ninth by Flgmstr Ottomar Haggenmüller up until his death on 5 December and the tenth by Ltn z S d R Karl-Heinrich Voss, who was killed in action on 17 December (*Greg VanWyngarden*)

on the 22nd at the hands of the recently commissioned Belgian ace Sous-Lt Thieffry.

On 10 September MFJ I withdrew to Coolkerke, southeast of Zeebrugge. The next day the unit logged three more successes, starting at 1210 hrs when Ltn z S Friedrich von Götz shot down Bristol F 2B A7187 of No 48 Sqn at Wyndaele, killing Sgt Harold Roebuck and 2Lt H T Batson. Flgmts Heinrich and Künstler each claimed a Camel near Schoore at 1910 hrs that evening, but the British recorded no corresponding loss, whereas von Götz was killed. He was probably flying the Albatros D V whose destruction over Leke was shared by Flt Lts Joseph S T Fall and Alfred W Wood and Flt Sub-Lt Harold F Stackard of 'Naval 9'.

This Albatros D V, turned over at Coolkerke, is believed to have been assigned to Theo Osterkamp. His preferred personal marking was two black bands separated by light yellow, which made his aeroplane look like a bumblebee (*Greg VanWyngarden*)

On 24 September Osterkamp brought SPAD VII S2466 down west of Westroosebeke. The French pilot, Capt Guy d'Aymery of *escadrille* SPA31, was taken prisoner.

On 1 October a new land-based fighter unit was formed at Neumünster to provide protection for the seaplanes patrolling the North Sea. Called *Seefrontstaffel Flandern*, abbreviated as *Seefrosta*, it was commanded by Ltn z S Hans Rolshoven and commenced operations on the 8th with 15 Albatros D IIIs, which were soon complemented by Pfalz D IIIs. A second *Marine Feld Jasta*, MFJ II, was organised at Coolkerke on the 15th, with Oblt z S Reusch as its commander and Ltn z S Osterkamp among its seconded cadre of experienced personnel.

Flgmt Heinrich of MFJ I claimed a SPAD south of Nieuwpoort and another west of Ramscapelle on 21 October, while Flgmt M Brenner downed a third scout southwest of Ramskapelle. British, French and Belgian records fail to identify any corresponding losses, however.

MFJ II suffered its first loss on 13 November when Flgmt Friedrich Heinze was brought down near Schoorbakke by Capt Bernard P G Beanlands of No 24 Sqn and captured. The British gave his lightning bolt-marked Ostdeutsche Albatros Werke-built Albatros D III Nr 2387/17 the captured aeroplane number G89. Ltn Siebel of the *Seefrosta* survived being downed in a Pfalz two days later. In contrast, Sachsenberg of MFJ I was credited with a Sopwith over Nieuwpoort on the 18th.

In spite of poor weather on 28 November, Ltn z S Rolshoven finally opened the *Seefrosta's* account by downing a 'DH 5' over Brugge. This may in fact have been a Camel of No 65 Sqn, which reported 2Lt J McKinnon last being seen in thick cloud over Zonnebeke during the dawn patrol. He was later determined to have been killed in action.

December began poorly for the naval fighters. Obflgmt Karl Meyer of the *Seefrosta* survived being shot down on the 3rd, but Flgmstr Ottomar Haggenmüller of MFJ II was killed north of Dixmude. He was undoubtedly the pilot of an Albatros with a black fuselage and white tail that attacked the hindmost Camel in a 'Naval 10' formation, only to be shot down in flames between Keyem and Leke by Flt Lt Wilfred A Curtis and Flt Sub Lt Frederick V Hall.

Obflgmstr Karl Meyer with Albatros Nr 5815/17 *Gussy*, which may have had a black-trimmed yellow fuselage band. After being reassigned to MFJ I on 20 June 1917, Meyer scored his eighth victory – a DH 4 from No 57 Sqn – on the 22nd. He later helped form the *Seefrontstaffel* on 16 October, but crashed on 28 December and died of his injuries in Leipzig three days later (*Greg VanWyngarden*)

On 12 December Ltn z S Karl-Heinrich Voss of MFJ I scored his first victory in the form of a Camel near Leke. Five days later, however, Voss was shot down in flames south of Pilkem by 2Lt Philip Kelsey of No 1 Sqn. The British registered the remains of his Albatros D V, Nr 2356/17, with the captured aeroplane number G100.

Sachsenberg was credited with a Sopwith two-seater destroyed northwest of Keyem on 18 December. That same day Flgmt Albin Bühl of the *Seefrosta* claimed a two-seater that went unconfirmed. He was promoted to Oberflugmaat following this mission. Both German claims for the 18th may have been over DH 4s of 5 Naval Squadron, whose mission that day was recorded by its leader, Flt Lt Charles P O Bartlett;

Seefrosta pilot Flgmt Albin Bühl, known as *'König'* (king) to his comrades, had at least two victories to his name when this photograph of him in his Albatros D Va was taken. The fighter seems to have had its landing gear beefed up. On 8 May 1917 he drove a DH 4 into the sea off Nieuwpoort, and subsequently scored an additional three victories with MFJ IV (*Greg VanWyngarden*)

'Eight of us, I leading in N6000, left at 1340 hrs for Engel aerodrome and ammunition dump. Sproatt led the three fighters. Formation good considering the raw element, and we crossed the lines north of Dixmude at 13,500 ft. Flak heavy and, near target, very accurate. All the Bessoneaux tents had been removed from the aerodrome, which appeared to be quite deserted, so we attacked the dump. Two formations of fighters came up at us on the way home and we put in some useful shooting at them at longish range. One formation of four, some 1500 ft above us, followed us to the lines, but they didn't seem anxious for a scrap. Sproatt, however, claimed to have shot an enemy aeroplane down in flames, and his gunlayer, Naylor, to have accounted for another from the first formation.'

'Naval 5' lost no DH 4s to match the German claims, but neither did the Marine *Jastas* lose any aeroplanes to match the two Albatros D Vs credited to the team of Flt Lt C D Sproatt and AGL Walter Naylor.

The next day Bühl officially opened his account with a double – a 'Handley Page' off Ostende and a DH 4 over Blankenberghe. The British lost no twin-engined Handley-Page O/100s that day, the German pilots possibly misidentifying a DH 4. In any case, Bühl's second victim was apparently DH 4 N6008 of 'Naval 5', crewed by Flt Sub-Lt S S Richardson and 1AC R A Furby. Flt Lt Bartlett, leading seven DH 4s to bomb Vlisseghem, described their fate;

'When off Middelkerke I suddenly observed what looked like a DH, some distance behind, going down in a vertical dive and, after a few seconds, there was a violent explosion and the whole aircraft disintegrated – a very nasty sight. I saw no sign of any attacking aircraft, nor were we experiencing any appreciable flak at the time. Richardson and gunlayer Furby failed to return, so it may have been them. Sproatt, however, claims to have shot down an enemy aeroplane in that area, and my impression was that it looked a bit small for a DH.'

Sproatt and Naylor were credited with a victory (Gunlayer Naylor's score would total 14 by war's end), but again there seems to have been some overclaiming on both sides.

A future naval ace got off to a false start when Ltn z S Paul Achilles of the *Seefrosta* was shot down between Brugge and Coxyde at 1235 hrs on 9 January 1918. His may have been one of two Albatros D IIIs that reportedly attacked Adj Jacques E Ledure and Lt Henri E Verelst of the *2éme Escadrille Belge* over Kerkhoek during a photographic mission between 1210-1310 hrs. Their Sopwith 1½ Strutter sustained multiple hits but made it back with two exposed plates.

On the 28th Flgmt Hans Groth of MFJ II was credited with a SPAD near Westende Bad, but the *Staffel* lost Flgmt Armin Undiener, killed over Snaeskerke. Their opponents may have been from the *5éme*

This evocative panoramic photograph shows Ltn z S Sachsenberg, in his chequer-banded Albatros D Va, leading MFJ I from Aertrycke aerodrome in early 1918. Taxiing to his right is Flgmstr Hans Goerth, his aeroplane boasting a white band inscribed with the name *LU* around its fuselage. A Pfalz D III of MFJ II can be seen second from right in the background (*Greg VanWyngarden*)

Escadrille Belge, which reported that Sous-Lt Baron Edmond Desclée was attacked by three Albatros over Terveate but was rescued by his squadronmate Sgt Charles de Montigny, who was not credited with a victory.

Winter dragged on with little of note to report until 9 March 1918, when 11 Naval Squadron staged a bombing raid that drew up both *Marine Jastas*. Ltn z S d R Anton Wessels of MFJ I was credited with a DH 4 between Nieuwpoort and Slype. This was probably the aeroplane of Flt Sub-Lt Bannatyne, who was wounded twice and his observer hit in the leg. Nevertheless, the crew managed to cross the frontlines and land on the beach at Coxyde. The Germans also engaged Camels over Booitschouke that same day, Flgmt Mayer of MFJ I being credited with one and Flgmt Kulbe of MFJ II getting a second, along with one 'forced to land' that was not confirmed. Vzflgmstr Hans Bossler of MFJ II was wounded in action.

On 11 March Heinrich downed DH 4 N5969 of 'Naval 2' near La Panne, Flt Sub-Lt C G McDonald and AM1 P J Clapp both being killed. Osterkamp of MFJ II scored his seventh victory – a Camel – three kilometres south of Pervyse on the 16th and Sachsenberg brought down a Breguet over Pervyse the next day.

On 21 March the Germans launched their *Kaiserschlacht* offensive in a last ditch bid for victory on the Western Front, and the air superiority task was primarily borne by the *Luftstreitskräfte's Jagdgeschwader* and *Jagdstaffeln*. A significant event for MFJ II on 21 March, however, was the reassignment of its CO, Oblt z S Reusch, to lead *Marine Schutz Staffel* I. Command of the *Jasta* duly passed to Ltn z S Osterkamp. MFJ I had an encounter with 'Naval 4' Camels the following day, and this resulted in the unit's top scorer, Heinrich, force landing near Vlisseghem wounded. His aeroplane was credited to Flt Lt Alexander M Shook.

On 24 March Flgmt Christian Kairies of the *Seefrosta* shot down Camel B3774 off Nieuwpoort, its pilot, Flt Sub-Lt L C Messiter of 13 Naval Squadron, being rescued. Born in Memel on 24 October 1896, Kairies had been a member of the *Seefrontstaffel* since its formation. Minutes after downing Messiter, Kairies was himself wounded and forced to crash-land his Pfalz D IIIa near Middelkerke by Flt Sub-Lt George C Mackay of 'Naval 13'. More would be heard from Kairies in coming months.

MFJ II sparked a sprawling melée at 1700 hrs on 26 March when Flgobmt Groth went after an Allied balloon. Camels of 'Naval 4' descended on him from 17,000 ft and Osterkamp in turn led the covering flight down on the British fighters. The engagement was also spotted by Sous-Lt André de Meulemeester of the *9éme Escadrille Belge,* and he too led his 'Yellow Flight' into the fray. de Meulemeester and his three

Theo Osterkamp stands beside an Albatros D Va in his 'bumblebee' stripes, which he pranged in the spring of 1918 (*Greg VanWyngarden*)

Hanriot HD 1 pilots reported engaging one out of a *Kette* of four Pfalz at 1737 hrs in a fight that twisted and turned its way from 4000 metres down to just 200 metres, at which point the German skilfully hedgehopped away, leaving the Belgians feeling both sick and impressed.

Canadian aces Flt Lt Ronald M Keirstead and Flt Sub-Lt Charles R R Hickey each claimed a Pfalz destroyed and one out of control in the fight. That evening Belgian headquarters received a copy of Keirstead's combat report, in which he claimed to have achieved his out of control in concert with the Belgian fighter pilots. As a consequence, Yellow Flight – de Meulemeester, Sous-Lt Gustave de Mévius and Adj Georges Kervyn de Lettenhove – were given joint credit. The three Belgian pilots stated, with no small degree of admiration for their aerobatic adversary, that the German had so outmanoeuvred them that they were sure that he had returned safely to his aerodrome. After a few days of back-and-forth arguing, Belgian HQ downgraded Yellow Flight's victory to a 'probable', although it stood as 'confirmed' for Keirstead.

On the German side, Osterkamp and Flgmt Eduard Blaas were each credited with a Camel. For all that, the only known casualty on either side was the would-be balloon-buster who instigated the fight. Groth, who came down at Pervyse in Pfalz D IIIa Nr 5923/17 and was captured, died of his wounds soon thereafter.

There were neither successes nor losses for the *Marine Jastas* on 1 April 1918, but the date bore some passing significance in that their frequent adversary, the RNAS, ceased to exist upon its amalgamation with the RFC into the new independent arm, the Royal Air Force. All RNAS squadrons were redesignated within the 200 numerical category. Their personnel, however, remained unchanged, and as dangerous as ever. There would be no similar merging of German *Marine* and *Luftstreiskräfte* units, but 3 April saw MFJ I and II stationed together at Jabbeke.

On 23 April the Royal Navy staged its Zeebrugge raid. During the course of the day's action Flgmstr Brenner of MFJ I drove a Sopwith down into the sea off Middelkerke for his fourth victory, but two of his squadronmates were injured in crashes. Osterkamp downed a Camel north of Ostende, while Flgmt Hans Goerth of MFJ I claimed a DH 4 at sea that would ultimately remain unconfirmed.

Two days later Sachsenberg downed a Sopwith two-seater over Avekapelle and Osterkamp a SPAD between Avekapelle and Pervyse, tying their respective scores at ten. The latter was probably *10éme Escadrille Belge* pilot Sgt Maj Charles Wouters, who was attacked by two enemy fighters but returned safely. Flgmt Stucke of MFJ II also claimed a Camel over Steenkerke on 25 April, although it was more likely a HD 1 of the *9éme Escadrille Belge*, which had a ten-minute engagement with an estimated

Flgobmt Gerhard Hubrich (left) poses with Bordwart Knörzer and two other groundcrewmen before his Albatros D Va Nr 5815/17. Flying in the *Seefrontstaffel* or *Seefrosta* at Neumunster, *'Kuken'* ('Chick') Hubrich was credited with a Sopwith Camel for his first victory on 4 May 1918 (*Alex Imrie via Mike O'Connor*)

30 enemy fighters. The Belgians lost no pilots, but Sous-Lt 'Papa Gusto' de Mévius and Adj Kervyn de Lettenhove sent Pfalz D IIIa Nr 5942/17 crashing into the yard of Ferme Groote Westhof at Booitshoucke, killing Flgomt Bruno Fietzmann.

The *Seefrosta* scored on 27 April, with Flgmt Bühl claiming a Camel over Middelkerke that was not confirmed and the CO, Rolshoven, downing one that was. The *Staffel* got into a bigger dogfight off the coast between Westende and Nieuwpoort at 1910 hrs on 4 May, with Ltn z S der R Rudolf Spies being credited with a seaplane and a Camel, Ltn z S Reinhold Poss bagging two Sopwith seaplanes and Flgmt Gerhard Hubrich downing a Camel.

Born on 30 July 1896, Hubrich had been an aviator before the war, enlisting in the navy at its start and qualifying as a military pilot in October 1914. He had served as a reconnaissance pilot until 1916, when he transferred to a unit test-dropping aerial torpedoes. Hubrich joined the *Seefrontstaffel* sometime in 1918, bringing with him the nickname of '*Küken*' ('Chick'), which inspired the personal marking on his aeroplanes.

Ltn z S Rolshoven died in a crash at Zeebrugge on 6 May, Ltn z S Poss taking his place in command of the *Seefrosta*. The unit added to its laurels on the 8th when Bühl drove a DH 4 into the sea off Nieuwpoort. That same day MFJ II's Ltn z S Weinert claimed another DH 4, Ltn z S Brockhoff was credited with a Sopwith off Pervyse and Osterkamp claimed to have shot a SPAD down into the sea, although this went unconfirmed. Sgt Albert Ferrat of French *escadrille* SPA80 was lost off Bray Dunes and Belgian SPAD pilot Sous-Lt Edmond Desclée of the *10éme Escadrille Belge* reported attacking four Albatros, although he was ultimately chased off by them.

Ltn z S Theodor Lodemann of the *Seefrosta* sent a Camel crashing into the sea off Ostende on 9 May, and although his victim remains unidentified, the Sopwith fighter that Osterkamp shot down off Breedene at 1702 hrs on 11 May was. His victim, Lt J Reid of No 213 Sqn, perished in B7192. Flgmstr Carl Kuring of MFJ II was credited with a 'Pup' on the 15th. Yet another MFJ II man, Flgmt Stucke, claimed a SPAD off Middelkerke on the 16th, but *Staffel* mate Flgmt Illig was wounded. Obmt Heinrich Hahn of MFJ I was also wounded and forced to land at Ghistelles.

Ltn z S Reinhold Poss, who on 7 May 1918 became leader of the second flight of the *Seefrontstaffel*, SFS II, poses in Albatros D Va Nr 7435/17. On 21 May he scored his third victory, over a Bristol F 2B, and on 28 June he downed a DH 4 of No 217 Sqn, followed by a DH 9 of No 218 Sqn on 16 July. Poss was himself forced to land near Mariakerke on 30 July after being shot up by a Camel (*Alex Imrie via Mike O'Connor*)

On 17 May Vzflgmstr d R Wilhelm Thöne joined MFJ I. Born on 22 January 1894, 'Willi' Thöne had been a machinist in 1913, prior to serving in the *Marine Infanterie* between 1914 and 1917. After qualifying as a pilot, he flew in MFFA II before transferring to fighters.

Poss and Lodemann of the *Seefrosta* each shot an F 2B of No 88 Sqn down into the sea off Mariakerke on 21 May, killing Lt G G Scobie and 2Lt F J D Hudson in B1341 and Lt K O Millar and

2Lt S Davidson in C839. Flgmt Held of MFJ II despatched a Camel over Ramskapelle that afternoon, while MFJ I claimed three successes – two DH 9s of No 211 Sqn to Sachsenberg and Flgmt Wagner and an F 2B downed at sea by Ltn z S Tinschert that was probably also from No 88 Sqn. Although the latter machine actually made it back to Allied lines, DH 9 B7661 came down in German territory, where 2Lts H E Tamsey and N B Harris were made PoWs. The second No 211 Sqn machine, B7604, returned to Allied lines with its crew, Lt R F C Metcalfe and 2Lt D R Bradley, unhurt.

Flgmt Bieber of the *Seefrosta* claimed two DH 4s on 24 May and Ltn z S d R Schultze of MFJ I was credited with another over Ostdunkerke-Bad on the 27th. The next morning Bieber brought down DH 4 A8065 of No 217 Sqn at Jehkooke at 0620 hrs, the wounded pilot, Lt Col P F M Fellows, and his gunner Sgt F N Prichard being made PoWs. Five minutes earlier, however, Ltn z S Johannes von Etzdorff had been killed over Wenduyne while attacking DH 9s.

Sachsenberg was credited with a DH 4 southwest of Nieuwekapelle on 29 May. This aeroplane may in fact have been a Sopwith 1½ Strutter of the *3éme Escadrille Belge*, whose crew, Adj Jean Meeûs and Lt Armand Ducellier, reported being attacked but were able to make Allied lines with the aid of their escorting Nieuport fighter, flown by 1Sgt René Gerard of the *4éme Escadrille Belge*. Thöne of MFJ I claimed a SPAD two-seater over the Nieuwpoort Mole the next day.

In June 1918, while the German army struggled to maintain the momentum of its offensive in France, the German navy's fighter force underwent significant expansion, as a new unit, MFJ III, was formed at Jabbeeke under the command of Ltn z S Brockhoff on the 23rd. Organised around a cadre of personnel drawn from MFJs I and II, including future aces Hans Goerth and Eduard Blaas, MFJ III joined those units within a new *Marine Jagdgruppe* headed by Ltn z S Sachsenberg. Like *Jagdgruppe* commanders in the *Luftstreitskräfte*, he continued to lead MFJ I as well.

Over the previous three weeks the veteran *Marine Jastas* had soldiered on. Flgmt Kuring of MFJ II started the month off by bringing down a DH 9 of No 98 Sqn near Ruidenberg, resulting in the capture of United States Air Service (USAS) pilot 2Lt L I A Peers, who had been attached to the RAF squadron, and his observer, Pte Wentworth. The next day MFJ I's Sachsenberg and Heinrich were each credited with a SPAD, but at 2100 hrs Flgmt Horst Sawatzki was wounded near Middelkerke. His was probably the Albatros D Va credited in flames to the F 2B team of Capt Allan Hepburn and 2AM Thomas Proctor of No 88 Sqn. On 3 June Flgmt Kairies of the *Seefrosta* brought down another No 98 Sqn DH 9 at Zuidschoote, the wounded pilot, Lt R A Bird, and his observer, Lt A R Cowan, becoming PoWs.

MFJ II came to the fore on 5 June with Osterkamp claiming a SPAD that was not confirmed (probably 1st Sgt Maj de Montigny of the *10éme Escadrille Belge*, who was forced to land at La Panne) and Flgmt Alexander Zenses downing a Camel east of Avekapelle that was. A Camel credited to Osterkamp near Ramskapelle on the 7th may have been Sgt Jean Van der Voordt of the *11éme Escadrille Belge*, who was attacked by an enemy fighter over Tervaete, separated from his six-Camel

German naval personnel examine a captured DH 9 at Zeebrugge. Although far from ideal as a bomber, the DH 9 was a frequent raider over German naval facilities in Flanders – and therefore a frequent victim of *Marine Feld Jasta* pilots – throughout 1918 (*Private collection of Milosz Zielinski*)

flight and chased back to the lines unscathed. Two days later MFJ II had the worst of its encounters, with Ltn z S Weinert wounded – possibly a Pfalz credited as out of control to Capt Solomon C Joseph of No 210 Sqn – and Ltn z S Heinrich Sattler killed at Langenhoek-Wadsland in Albatros D Va Nr 7265/17.

Aside from acquiring a third *Jagdstaffel* on 23 June, the *Marine Jagdgruppe* achieved nothing further until the 25th, when a succession of escorted bombing raids by the RAF suddenly heated things up over the Flanders coastline. On that day Flgmstr Wagner of MFJ I forced down DH 4 C2176 of No 211 Sqn off Ostende, from which the wounded pilot, 2Lt F Daltry, was taken prisoner but AG R Shepherd was killed. Ltn z S Schultze of MFJ II also claimed a SPAD off Wenanger.

Another raid on the 27th resulted in Flgmt Kutschke of the *Seefrosta* claiming a DH 4 and MFJ II adding four victories to its tally. Zenses destroyed DH 9 D5687 of No 218 Sqn off Zeebrugge, killing Lt C Briggs and 2Lt H W H Warner, while off Wenduyne Flgmt Bottler downed a DH 4 of No 202 Sqn, Osterkamp and Zenses were each credited with a Camel and Flgmt Stucke claimed another Camel that went unconfirmed. The Allied fighters were probably Belgian aeroplanes, whose pilots reportedly had a lively engagement with Pfalz scouts 3800 metres over the Houthulst Forest. Sous-Lt de Meulemeester of the *9éme Escadrille Belge* had to disengage with a gun jam and Adj Willy Heyvaert of the *11éme Escadrille Belge* crash-landed on the Furnes-Houthulst road, suffering minor injuries in the process.

Poss of the *Seefrosta* started the 28th off at 0700 hrs by despatching DH 4 A8023 into the sea off Westende – Lt A E Bingham and 2Lt L J Smith of No 217 Sqn were recovered as PoWs. At 2055 hrs that evening Osterkamp and Zenses of MFJ II were each credited with a two-seater south of Blankartsee, Osterkamp's apparently being F 2B C4880 of No 88 Sqn, in which 2Lt J P West and AG A J Loton were killed.

On 29 June Flgmt Kähler and Ltn z S Lodemann of the *Seefrosta* each downed a DH 4 between St André and Varssenaere, while Flgmstr Wagner and Ltn z S Wessels of MFJ I claimed a Camel apiece. MFJ II's

Flgmt Kulbe was credited with a kite balloon six kilometres west of Oostkerke and the Belgians reported their balloon No 6 coming under attack, forcing Sgts Dohy and Puissant to take to their parachutes. The kite balloon was not destroyed, however. Osterkamp and Zenses of MFJ II also downed F 2Bs at Pervyse and southeast of Dixmude, respectively. These were again from No 88 Sqn, but both came down in Allied territory. C983's crew (Capt K R Simpson and Sgt Charles Hill) escaped without injury, and 2Lt Robert J Cullen, although wounded, brought D8022 over the lines with his observer, 2Lt Edward H Ward, unhurt.

MFJ I had another encounter with DH 4s and Camels on 30 June, during which Flgmt Borschert claimed a bomber over Blankenberghe and Vzflgmstr Thöne destroyed two Camels of No 204 Sqn, killing Lts J M Wilson in D3359 and S Harston in D3361. Zenses and Goerth of MFJ III also claimed DH 4s off Mariakerke, although only one was actually destroyed – A8013, in which Lt Clifford J Moir and Pte Edwin E Hunnisett of No 98 Sqn were killed.

German activity in July focused on the final push across the Marne. On 4 July, however, the *Seefrosta* had Ltn z S Theodor Lodemann killed following an engagement over Ypres, while Flgmt Clemens Kähler survived a crash landing at Thourout. The next day Flgmt Kulbe of MFJ II downed a DH 4 off Ostende, and on the 7th Flgmt Goerth forced DH 9 D1730 to crash into the sea off Nieuwpoort, killing Lt J R Harrington and 2Lt C L Bray of No 206 Sqn. On 10 July *Seefrosta* Albatros D Va Nr 7322/17 was downed near Kenberge – pilot Flgmt Eduard Schwarz died of his wounds at Blankenberghe four days later.

The *Marine Jagdgruppe* intercepted another bombing attack by No 211 Sqn on 13 July, with Sachsenberg scoring his 15th victory over a SPAD, although the *11éme Escadrille Belge* only reported four of its pilots being chased off by a larger formation of German fighters between Middelkerke and Westende. Nearby, MFJ III's Flgmt Blaas sent DH 9 B9346 crashing into the sea off Westduyne, killing 2Lt W J Gilman and Pte W J Atkinson, and Flgmt Ludewig was credited with the destruction of a second DH 9 off Middelkerke, which in fact made it home with the observer, 2Lt C W T Colman, wounded. Flgmt Held of MFJ II was credited with a SPAD off Ostende at 0850 hrs the next morning, but the Belgians only reported three Hanriots of their *9éme Escadrille Belge* engaging four Fokkers over Merckem, with no loss to either side.

On 16 July, while the German army made its last, ultimately failed, attempts to force its way over the Marne, a succession of bombing attacks by Nos 202 and 218 Sqns in Flanders brought up the *Marine Jastas* in force. At 1230 hrs Poss of SFS II claimed a DH 9 over Zeebrugge. Sachsenberg drove a SPAD into the sea off Zeebrugge at 1415 hrs, followed by a DH 4 at 1420 hrs and another over Middelkerke five minutes later, while Ltn z S Wessels of MFJ I claimed a DH 9 again over Middelkerke. Goerth of MFJ III finished a busy day by downing DH 4 A7868 of No 202 Sqn north of Zevecoote at 1825 hrs, killing Lts Lionel A Ashfield – a six-victory ace with the DFC – and M G English.

MFJ II had a spirited dogfight over Nieuwpoort at 1020 hrs on 20 July, with Osterkamp, Zenses and Bottler each adding a Camel to their tallies. Flgmstr Alfons Nitsche, however, was shot down and killed

Besides being credited with at least five victories Willy Thöne of MFJ I survived two crash landings – on 31 July 1918, when he was probably shot down by Lt Archie Buchanan of No 210 Sqn, and the second sometime in August when, after his engine was hit by groundfire, he crashed just off the Flanders coast and waded ashore (Greg VanWyngarden)

near Leffinghe in Fokker D VII Nr 506/18, probably by Capt Harold T Mellings of No 210 Sqn, and Flgmt Kuring was forced to land in Fokker D VII Nr 612/18 by another No 210 Sqn pilot. Two days later, Zenses was lightly wounded by anti-aircraft fire between Ostende and Oudenburg, but he remained with MFJ II while recuperating.

The *Jagdgruppe* had another encounter around Pervyse on 25 July, with Lt z S Wessels of MFJ I claiming two Camels, Sachsenberg bagging another and Osterkamp of MFJ II downing a fourth south of Nieuwpoort. On the 29th Osterkamp and Zenses each claimed a DH 4 south of Oudenkapelle, while Flgmstr Ledy claimed a Camel. Only Osterkamp's was confirmed, but even that DH 4, D8402, made it home with its crew, Lt W Chalaire and Pvt A E Humphrey, wounded.

July ended dubiously for the naval units. Vzflgmstr Bottler's claim against a two-seater on the 30th was not confirmed, while Ltn z S Wieland of the *Seefrosta* was wounded, having possibly become the sixth, and last, victory for Capt Maurice L Cooper of No 213 Sqn. On the 31st Willi Thöne of MFJ I claimed another No 213 Sqn Camel before his engine was hit and he crash landed, miraculously emerging from the wreckage uninjured. His may have been the Fokker 'destroyed' northwest of Wervicq that day by Lt Archie Buchanan of No 210 Sqn.

August began with the *Seefrosta* being divided into distinct flights or *Ketten*, namely SFS 1 and 2, and receiving its first Fokker D VIIs. Kuring of MFJ II was credited with a single-seater on 1 August, but Zenses was wounded in Fokker D VII Nr 610/18 – he was probably the seventh, and final, victory for Lt Albert L Jones of No 210 Sqn. When a German kite balloon broke loose on the 3rd, Flgmt Held of MFJ II destroyed it over Wenduyne.

There was some cause for celebration on 5 August when Sachsenberg was awarded the *Orden Pour le Mérite*, making him only the second naval

Oblt z S Sachsenberg's men throw a party on the occasion of his being awarded the *Orden Pour le Mérite* at Jabbeke on 12-13 August 1918. Identified personnel have been numbered as follows – 1. Vzflgmt Karl Sharon, MFJ II (8 victories), 4. Vzflgmt Hans Goerth, MFJ III (7 victories), 5. Vzflgmstr Carl Kuring, MFJ II (4 victories), 7. Ltn z S Heinrich Wessels, MFJ I (6 victories), 9. Ltn z S Wilhelm Thöne, MFJ I (5 victories), 10. *Gruppenkommandeur* Sachsenberg (31 victories), 11. Ltn z S Bertram Heinrich, MFJ I (12 victories), 12. Vzflgmstr Hechner, MFJ I, Ltn z S Theo Osterkamp, MFJ II (32 victories), 15. Flgmt Wilhelm Grabowski, MFJ I, 16. Flgmt Horst Sawatzki, MFJ I, and 17. Ltn z S Phillip Becht, MFJ I (4 victories). The night's festivities were followed the next day by a sobering morning (*Alex Imrie via Mike O'Connor*)

airman to receive it after Christiansen. Over the next week the *Marine Jastas* remained sidelined, while to the south, around Amiens, the British launched a devastatingly well-planned counteroffensive on the 8th which Gen Erich von Ludendorff would proclaim 'The Black Day of the German Army'.

On 10 August the *Marine Jagdgruppe* received its first specimens of a promising new fighter, the Fokker E V parasol monoplane. The unit had little time to test the new aeroplanes out, however, before a succession of Allied bombing strikes over Flanders precipitated a concurrent burst of naval fighter activity.

Oblt z S Sachsenberg, second from right, stands before his Fokker E V, which apparently had its fuselage covered in his yellow and black diamonds livery, as well as having some eyes painted on the cowling. Visiting Halberstadt chief engineer Karl Theis is second from left. Sachsenberg may have been flying the 'monoplane' reported in a dogfight with the American 17th Aero Squadron on 14 August in which Ltn z S Hans Goldenstedt of MFJ I fatally collided with 1Lt Lyman E Case and 2Lt William H Shearman was made a PoW, later dying of his wounds (*Greg VanWyngarden*)

Thöne of MFJ I started 12 August off by claiming a 'Camel' over Poelkapelle at 0845 hrs – possibly an HD 1 of the *9éme Escadrille Belge*, which engaged five Fokkers at that time but suffered no losses – and downed another over Wenduyne at 1140 hrs, wounding Capt John E L Hunter of No 204 Sqn. At about the same time SFS 2's Flgmt Kähler claimed a Camel near Wenduyne and Ltn z S d R Spies downed one over Middelkerke, resulting in No 204 Sqn's Lt Richard A C Hill being killed and Lt S C J Akin captured.

Sachsenberg sent a Camel crashing into the sea off Ostende at 1253 hrs, killing 1Lt Ralph D Gracie of the 17th Aero Squadron USAS, followed two minutes later by DH 9 D1691 of No 218 Sqn. The pilot of the latter machine, US Navy Ens George C Moseley (a former Lafayette Flying Corps fighter pilot with *escadrille* N150, now temporarily assigned to the RAF), brought the aeroplane down in Allied lines, with his observer, Lt M M Lowry, unhurt. Hubrich of SFS 1 downed Camel D9648 of No 204 Sqn over Westende at 1310 hrs, its pilot, Lt W A Pomeroy, force landing at Mardyke unhurt.

At 2000 hrs that evening Ltn z S Max Stinsky of SFS 1 downed a Camel near Middelkerke, and during the next hour Osterkamp claimed three victories, of which one, a Camel over Ramskapelle at 2050 hrs, was confirmed. Its wounded pilot, 1Lt Harriss B Alderman of the 17th Aero Squadron, made it to Allied lines.

All in all it had been an exceptional day, and the *Marine Jagdflieger* gathered at Snelleghem that night for a celebration full of *'Wein, Weib und Gesang'*. There were no doubt some hangovers the next morning, but nothing to match the reprisal that the RAF visited on Jabbeeke at 0640 hrs. Camels of the 17th Aero Squadron bombed and strafed the aerodrome, after which DH 9s of No 211 Sqn gave it a more substantial pounding. The result was a hangar demolished, a barracks damaged, two Fokker D VIIs destroyed by fire, ten more completely wrecked and five damaged. Flgmstr Wilhelm Grabowski of MFJ II was mortally wounded and Flgmstr Wilhelm Drews and Vzflgmstr

Günther Knie of MFJ III were killed, along with groundcrewman Flugzeugmechaniker Friedrich Schramm.

Taking off seeking vengeance, Sachsenberg claimed two victories that day, but neither one was confirmed. SFS 2 intercepted more bombers over Dixmude at 1715 hrs, Ltn z S Achilles and Flgmt Kairies each being credited with a DH 9 destroyed. No 211 Sqn lost only one of its aeroplanes, however, and Ltn z S Spies was wounded in the engagement.

MFJ I took some revenge on the 17th Aero Squadron on 14 August, when Ltn z S Werner Bastian and Flgmt Hermann Hackbusch were credited with two of its Camels downed over Oostkamp, but at the cost of Flgmt Karl Goldenstedt, who was killed. A Fokker was jointly credited to 1Lt Lloyd A Hamilton, 1Lt Jesse F Campbell and 2Lt Robert M Todd, while 1Lt Glenn D Wicks was awarded another. The latter reported;

'While on patrol cooperating with bombers, we encountered a flight of six Fokker biplanes and one monoplane. One dived on the formation, turning into me from the rear. I pulled round and fired about 75 rounds from 50 ft. I saw tracers going into the fuselage. The enemy aeroplane went over my head and, without attempting to pull up, flew straight into the Camel behind me. The Camel's tail was smashed and the enemy aeroplane's left lower wing was torn off. Both machines went straight down, flopping about.'

Goldenstedt apparently collided with 1Lt Lyman E Case, who was also killed, while 2Lt William H Shearman was taken prisoner but subsequently died of his wounds. The 'monoplane' Wicks reported to be accompanying the D VIIs might have been flown by Sachsenberg, who had taken a swift liking to the new Fokker E V.

The friendly rivalry between the *Marine Jagdgruppe's* leading aces came to the fore on 16 August, as Sachsenberg drove a Camel of No 213 Sqn into the sea off Zeebrugge and then disabled the already flak-damaged DH 9 B7623 of No 211 Sqn, resulting in 1Lt Donald R Harris USAS and 2Lt James Munro force landing in the Netherlands, where they were interned. A second DH 9 (C6348) splashed into the sea off Weilingen, where the Dutch rescued Capt R M Wynne-Eaton and 2Lt T B Dodwell, the wounded observer having to have an arm amputated. Sachsenberg was credited with his 23rd victory. That same day Osterkamp downed DH 9 D1708 of No 218 Sqn for his 22nd success, its crew, Lt A C Lloyd and 2Lt M G Wilson, also being interned by the Dutch.

Also on 16 August, Ltn Ernst Riedel of *Jasta* 19 was killed while testing a Fokker E V. Three days later, Ltn Emil Rolff of *Jasta* 6 died the same way. The wing failures that caused these tragedies were attributed to structural rot due to Fokker's notoriously poor quality control,

Vzfmstr Hans Goerth had three credited victories to his name when he posed beside his Fokker E V, one of two (Nrs 144/18 and 155/18) delivered to MFJ III on 10 August 1918. He would score four more times by war's end, but not in the 'Parasol' (*Greg VanWyngarden*)

and until the problem was remedied, all E Vs – including those assigned to the *Marine Feld Jastas* – were grounded.

Osterkamp claimed a DH 9 off Breedene on 21 August, but again the pilot, Lt G R Hurst of No 202 Sqn, got his wounded observer, Sgt L A Allen, safely to Allied territory. SFS 1's Ltn z S Eberhard Crantz, along with *Staffel* mates Flgmt Hubrich and Ltn z S Phillip Becht, as well as MFJ I's Ltn z S Sachsenberg, all claimed DH 4s too, although Allied records fail to identify them. Kairies and Hubrich were also credited with an escorting Camel each, corresponding to No 213 Sqn's Lt J Wooding, brought down and taken prisoner, and Lt W A Rankin, who force landed unhurt in Allied lines.

The *Seefrosta* suffered a loss of its own when Fokker D VII Nr 885/18 was shot down off Blankenberghe by Lt William E Gray of No 213 Sqn, who reported that the pilot jumped or fell from his aeroplane into the sea. Flgmt Friedrich Gröschke's body washed ashore a few days later in the Netherlands, and local authorities informed Berlin and buried him with military honours.

On 23 August Osterkamp downed a Camel off Pervyse and Ltn z S Heinrich of MFJ I was credited with a DH 4 over Booitshoucke for his 12th victory. Kairies of SFS 2 'made ace' two days later with a Camel off Blankenberghe and a second over Ichteghem, bringing his total to six, but No 213 Sqn recorded only one loss – Lt E C Toy, killed in C6358.

MFJ II intercepted a bombing raid over Ostende on 30 August, with Osterkamp and Vzflgmstr Karl Scharon being awarded probables and Flgmt Illig of MFJ II being credited with a DH 9. Vzflgmstr Goerth of MFJ III claimed his fifth success by downing Camel D9482 over Handzame, killing 2Lt H G Pike of No 65 Sqn. It was MFJ I's turn to mourn the next day, however, as Ltn z S Werner Bastian and Bertram Heinrich were killed fighting more Camels over Thourout. Heinrich was probably the fourth of an eventual 12 victories for Canadian Lt William S Jenkins of No 210 Sqn.

As the Allies regrouped their forces for new offensives in September – including a push into Flanders – the German naval fighter force underwent a final spurt of growth on the first day of the month when the *Seefrontstaffel's* two *Ketten* were expanded into *Jagdstaffeln*, MFJ IV and V. Sachsenberg scored his 25th victory the next day and then departed on a well-earned leave. Osterkamp led the *Marine Jagdgruppe* and Ltn z S Becht commanded MFJ I in his absence.

Ltn z S Brockhoff of MFJ III was credited with a DH 4 over Furnes on 3 September, and on the 5th Flgmt Mayer of MFJ II brought down Camel D1824 near Stahlhille, 2Lt C E Francis of No 213 Sqn being taken prisoner. At 1750 hrs that afternoon Flgmt Karl Engelfried opened MFJ V's account with DH 4 C1224 west of Knocke, its crew, Lt J G

Another promising new design that caught pilots' attention in 1918 was the Siemens-Schuckert Werke D IV. Ltn z S Bertram Heinrich of MFJ I had as many as 12 victories to his name when he posed with Nr 3028/18, but on 31 August he was shot down and killed in a Fokker D VII, probably by Lt William S Jenkins of No 210 Sqn (*Greg VanWyngarden*)

Munro and 2Lt T W Brodie of No 218 Sqn, force landing in the Netherlands.

On 15 September Ltn z S Poss, commanding MFJ IV, shot down Camel E4418 off Zeebrugge at 1510 hrs, killing Lt R C Pattulo of No 204 Sqn. When Nos 211 and 218 Sqns came over on a bombing raid, they were intercepted at 1705 hrs, resulting in DH 9s being credited to Vzflgmstr Hackbusch and Ltn z S Freymadl of MFJ I and Flgmt Kutschke and Engelfried of MFJ V. The actual British casualties amounted to DH 9 D3210 of No 211 Sqn being shot up, but 2Lt J M Payne making it home with his wounded observer, Lt C T Linford, and C2158 of No 218 Sqn force landing in Holland. The latter aeroplane had been zealously pursued by Engelfried, who also ended up force landing in Fokker D VII Nr 5584/18 to join his injured victims, Lt W S Mars and 2Lt H E Power, in Dutch internment. He managed to escape soon afterward, however, and rejoined his unit.

The *Marine Feld Jastas'* private war with their former RNAS counterparts raged anew on 16 September, starting with a Camel credited to Goerth of MFJ III over Zerkeghen at 0915 hrs. His victim, 18-year-old 2Lt Edward B Markquick, had only been in No 210 Sqn ten days before he died. At 1110 hrs the Germans again encountered No 210 Sqn, with Osterkamp being credited with two Camels and Ltn z S Curt Wilhelm of MFJ IV getting one. The only British loss, 2Lt Jack A Lewis, had been with the squadron a month prior to being killed in Camel D3357. During a last encounter over Blankenberghe at 1900 hrs, nine of No 204 Sqn's pilots claimed three two-seaters and eight Fokkers in 15 minutes, but the only German naval casualties were Vzflgmstr Horst Sawatzki and Flgmt Nake of MFJ I, both lightly wounded.

'Küken' Hubrich of MFJ IV scored his fifth success, over a Camel, on 17 September. On the 20th, elements of the original *Staffeln* took advantage of Lt George E C Howard leading his flight of No 204 Sqn Camels at low altitude and failing to watch for the 'Hun in the sun'. While the RAF pilots claimed six Fokkers, Camels were credited to Becht of MFJ I and Osterkamp, Stinsky and Scharon of MFJ II. Actual losses were 2Lt C Leonard Kelly, killed by Osterkamp, and 2Lt Ernest G Rolph, who was captured after being downed by Becht. Stinsky reported his Camel crashing in Allied lines southeast of Pervyse, its pilot, Lt D F Tysoe, being wounded.

Flgmt Karl Schiffmann of MFJ IV was shot down and killed over Ichteghem, east of Dixmude, on the 23rd. Ironically, in view of the epidemic of overclaiming that pervaded the British forces, a claim by a No 213 Sqn patrol that it had driven a Fokker down out of control six miles east of Dixmude was disallowed by wing HQ!

The new *Staffeln* strode to the fore over the next few days. On 24 September Ltn z S Wilhelm of MFJ IV was credited with a

Ltn z S Eberhard Cranz of MFJ V poses with his damaged Fokker D VII. At far right is Ltn z S Paul Achilles, who after a modest start in *Seefrosta* II distinguished himself with MFJ V in the final months of the war, his eighth victory being one of four French kite balloons claimed by the naval *Jagdflieger* on 26 October 1918 (*Greg VanWyngarden*)

Camel over Pervyse, although his wounded victim, Capt Solomon C Joseph of No 210 Sqn, made it to Allied lines. Ltn z S Achilles, now with MFJ V, brought down DH 9 D7208 of No 108 Sqn at Werckem, 2Lt J M Dandy and Sgt C P Crites becoming PoWs. In a fight on the 25th with No 213 Sqn, which claimed one Fokker destroyed, Vzflgmstr Zenses of MFJ II downed one Camel and Achilles of MFJ V got two, killing 2Lt J C Sorley and Lt L C Scroggie, and bringing Lt C P Sparks down as a PoW.

Engelfried and Kairies of MFJ V each downed a No 204 Sqn Camel at 1030 hrs on 26 September, killing 2Lt G E C Howard and Lt William B Craig (the latter a Canadian ace with eight victories). MFJ I had two successes over Ostende at 1115 hrs when Freymandl destroyed DH 4 A7632 of No 202 Sqn, killing Lt F A B Gasson and 2Lt S King, and Sawatzki brought down Camel E1552, 2Lt W R Thornton of No 65 Sqn becoming a PoW.

The long awaited Allied offensive in Flanders, the Fourth Battle of Ypres, began on 28 September, with Gen Sir Herbert Plumer's Second Army and the Belgian army retaking the Houthulst Forest during the course of the day. The German navy's sideshow war on the Flanders coast was now a critical front.

Osterkamp and Zenses of MFJ II commenced the day's hostilities by downing a Camel each over Woumen at 1230 hrs. Their adversaries from No 204 Sqn only lost one of their number, however, with Lt R McI Gordon making it back to Allied lines despite being wounded. Flgmt Nake of MFJ I brought down DH 4 A8025 near Leke at 1430 hrs, Capt A V Bowater and Lt D L Melvin becoming PoWs. Poss and 'König' Bühl of MFJ IV were each credited with a Sopwith Dolphin over Roulers at 1745 hrs, but No 79 Sqn lost only one aeroplane, whose American pilot, Lt R J Morgan, became a PoW.

MFJ II scored the rest of the day's victories, Flgmt Pfeiffer claiming a Camel at Woumen and Ltn z S Hermann Bargmann a DH 9 near Beerst at 1815 hrs. Pfeiffer's likely victim, Lt Risdon McKenzie Bennett of No 204 Sqn, had scored his fifth victory 12 days earlier. Also reported slain by flak over Thorout, the 18-year-old Bennett was the youngest ace to lose his life during the war. Bergmann's DH 9 was possibly from No 218 Sqn, which lost the aeroplane crewed by US Marines 1Lt Everett R Brewer and GSgt Harry B Wershiner. They were credited with downing a Fokker – the first aerial victory credited to the US Marine Corps – before coming down in Allied lines seriously wounded.

Meanwhile, at 1810 hrs, Osterkamp claimed a Breguet 14A2 for his 27th victory. Adj Robert Cajot and Lt Alfred Bricoult of the *2éme Escadrille Belge* were artillery spotting over the Cortemarck railway station when they came under attack from four Fokkers. Bricoult expended all of his ammunition in the action and claimed an adversary out of control before the Breguet was driven down in flames. Miraculously, both crewmen survived to become PoWs.

Fighting was no less intense on 29 September, as Freymandl, Hackbusch and Flgmt Riess of MFJ I were each credited with a Camel over Oostkamp at 0820 hrs. Flgmt Blaas of MFJ III got another Camel over Oudecapelle at 1205 hrs and Osterkamp finished the day with another Breguet west of Zarren, which was more likely a SPAD two-seater

Albatros-built Fokker D VIIs at Jabbeke aerodrome in October 1918. The second aeroplane from the left is Flgmstr Hans Goerth's Nr 5492/18 of MFJ III, and the fourth from right seems to have the chick emerging from its egg marking that played on the nickname of Flgmt Gerhard 'Kuken' Hubrich, who brought his total to eight while serving with MFJ IV (*Fleet Air Arm Museum JMB/GSL08302*)

of French *escadrille* SPA34, which reported MdL Bellencourt and Sous-Lt de François Le Clerk de Bussy down in Allied lines wounded.

A bombing raid by No 108 Sqn ran into a 'naval buzz saw' over Houthulst on 1 October, with DH 9s falling to Blaas and Goerth of MFJ III and one to Poss of MFJ IV. Two crews were killed, while DH 9 F5847 returned to Allied territory badly shot up with 2Lts C S Whellock and J W White wounded. Hubrich of MFJ IV claimed another DH 9 southeast of Roulers, while Blaas and Goerth despatched two escorting Camels of No 210 Sqn, killing Maj R S G Sibley and 2Lt R W Johnson. Kutschke of MFJ V claimed a DH 9 over Roulers, while Achilles of MFJ V and Ltn z S Fischer of MFJ III were credited with a Camel each – possibly from the *11éme Escadrille Belge*, whose Lt Louis Wouters crashed his aeroplane after a combat near Bulscamp but emerged uninjured.

In contrast to the new units, MFJ I did not start October off well, two of its pilots, Ltn z S Freymadl and Flgmt Berndt, being wounded in action. Moreover, MFJ V lost one of its aces when Flgmt Christian Kairies was shot down by a No 210 Sqn Camel and taken prisoner, dying of his wounds in the hospital at Zeebrugge the next day.

MFJ II intercepted DH 9s of No 206 Sqn over Roulers on 3 October, Vzflgmstr Zenses being credited with two and Flgmstr Kuring a third. The only squadron loss, however, was DH 9 F1159, whose observer, Cpl A F Bailey, was killed and the wounded pilot, Sgt R Walker, taken prisoner. Ltn Hermann Meyer of MFJ IV was killed that day, his aeroplane possibly being one of two Fokkers credited to Capt Walter M Carlaw of No 70 Sqn as destroyed over Roulers.

Only a handful of actions occurred over the next few days. Scharon was credited with a Camel and a DH 9 on 7 October, Sachsenberg returned from leave the next day and Hubrich claimed a Dolphin over Zarren on the 9th. At about this time all five *Marine Feld Jastas* were officially organised into a *Marine Feld Jagdgeschwader* under Sachsenberg's overall leadership. Consequently, Ltn z S Becht's temporary command of MFJ I became permanent.

A sortie against the Allied balloon line by MFJs II and IV on 14 October became a major air battle when it drew the attention of perennial adversary No 213 Sqn, as well as Dolphins from No 79 Sqn. MFJ II's Vzflgmstr Scharon downed a Camel between Roulers and Cortemarck, while Zenses was credited with a Camel, a Dolphin and the balloon at Staden. MFJ IV did even better, with Bühl obtaining his fifth victory over a Dolphin, Offstv Hoffknecht downing another, Hubrich credited with a Dolphin and a Camel and Poss accounting for two Camels and a balloon over the Houthulst Forest. That totalled 11 naval victories out of the 38 claimed by all German fighter pilots that day, albeit at the cost of Ltn z S Max Stinsky killed in action.

No fewer than six Camel pilots of No 213 Sqn were killed in the action, namely 2Lts W T Owen, F R L Allen, J C J McDonald and E B McMurty, as well as attached US Navy pilot Lt Kenneth McLeish and Canadian ace Capt John E Greene, who was credited with his 15th victory (a Fokker out of control in concert with McLeish) before he died. However, No 79 Sqn logged no losses, while claiming five Fokkers.

That same day the Belgians had kite balloon No 85 destroyed, its observer parachuting safely, and the *11éme Escadrille Belge* fought several combats with Fokkers over the Houthulst Forest. *Marine Feld* pilots also reported a balloon of the French *74e Compagnie d'Aérostières* going down in flames northeast of Houthulst, after which the *4e Escadrille* SPAD XI team of Lts Henri Crombez and Paul du Roy de Blicquy shot down its attacker, Fokker D VII Nr 4033/18, which turned over upon landing in their lines and was subsequently photographed. Since Stinsky came down at Snelleghem, near his aerodrome at Jabbeeke, and the Germans recorded no other losses in the area, this captured aeroplane presents something of a mystery.

On 15 October the German army was in full retreat in Flanders and the *Marine Feld Jastas* bore the brunt of the day's air action, with Zenses and Scharon claiming a Dolphin each over Roulers – their 15th and fifth victories, respectively – while Sachsenberg's Camel victory over Hooglede remained unconfirmed. Their opponents were probably Belgian. In a dogfight pitting five SPAD XIIIs of the *10éme Escadrille Belge* and three Camels of the *11éme Escadrille Belge* against 12 to 15 Fokker D VIIs, Sgt Jean van der Voordt of the latter unit claimed a Fokker that dived straight into the ground, while squadronmate Sgt Léon Guillon drove a Fokker with a yellow band on the fuselage down out of control before his attention was distracted by two more attacking D VIIs.

Adj Charles de Montigny of the *10éme Escadrille Belge* also brought down a Fokker before he was wounded and forced to crash land in Allied lines. He eventually succumbed to his injuries on 30 October. The *10éme Escadrille Belge's* commander, Lt Louis Robin, also went into a dive during the course of the fighting, suggesting that his and de Montigny's SPADs were the 'Dolphins' claimed by Zenses and Scharon. Sachsenberg's victim – apparently an HD 1 – actually crashed, but the pilot, Capt Paul G J Hiernaux of the *11éme Escadrille Belge*, emerged from the wreckage unhurt.

The Belgians exacted a toll on the enemy this time, however. MFJ V lost Flgobmt Schönbaum, who was wounded, and Flgmt Baum landed his damaged aeroplane in Holland and was interned. A worse loss was van der Voort's victim, 11-victory ace and *Staffelführer* Reinhold Poss, who was captured. Ltn z S Carl Wilhelm took command of MFJ IV.

Bad weather then brought a relative lull in activity, although Ltn z S Achilles of MFJ V downed a DH 9 north of Bellem on 22 October, killing Lt C F Cave and 2Lt H McNish of No 108 Sqn. Favourable weather the next day brought a bombing raid that cost No 108 Sqn another DH 9, and the lives of Capt G C Hayes and 2Lt G Brown, to Sachsenberg's guns, but the main event pitted the *Geschwader* CO and MFJ II against escorting Camels. Sachsenberg was credited with two fighters destroyed, Zenses with three and Scharon and Ltn z S Horst Merz with one apiece.

Against those seven Camel claims, No 204 Sqn actually lost five aeroplanes, with all their pilots being killed – Capt Thomas W Walsh, Lt Frederick G Bayley, Sgt C M A Mahon, Lt Oliver J Orr (an American in RAF service who had scored his fifth victory nine days earlier) and attached USAS member 2Lt Geoffrey Sutcliffe. Among No 204 Sqn's claims was a Fokker out of control by 2Lt Henry G Clappison, while 19-year-old Lt John D Lightbody, from Hamilton, Scotland, reported being attacked by three Fokkers that drove him down to 100 ft. At this point he executed a sharp turn and looked back to see two of his pursuers collide and fall to the ground in pieces. Lightbody was credited with the unusual double victory, this collision possibly resulting in the death of one of his opponents, Ltn z S Hermann Bargmann of MFJ II.

On 26 October the French *VIe Armée* advanced in Flanders, to which the naval *Jastas* responded with a sortie against the French balloon line at, and adjacent to, Deinze. Becht of MFJ I, Brockhoff of MFJ III and Achilles and Engelfried of MFJ V were each credited with a gasbag. Only two, from the *74e* and *85e Compagnies d'Aérostières*, actually burned, the other two being riddled with bullets. All the crewmen (Sous-Lts Bernardi, Ragué and Bruyère, Sgt Monteaux and Asp Martin) parachuted to safety. Sachsenberg also claimed a Camel over Essenghem, which may have been one from the *11éme Escadrille Belge*, which engaged three Fokkers near Ghent but lost no aeroplanes.

MFJ II encountered Camels over Deinze on 27 October, two of which were shot down by Zenses and Scharon, completing their scoring at 19 and eight, respectively. Royal Saxon *Jasta* 40's Ltns Carl Degelow and Willy Rosenstein also downed Camels over Wynghene, which combined with MFJ II's successes struck four more pilots from No 204 Sqn's rolls – 2Lt N Smith, who was captured, and 2Lts P F Cormack, A J F Ross and H G Murray, all of whom were killed. Sachsenberg destroyed a DH 9 over Deinze the next day, and scored his 31st, and final, victory on the 29th. Flgmt Wasserthal of MFJ IV finished the month with a DH 9 over Deinze on 30 October.

Becht of MFJ I was credited with a two-seater on 1 November, while Wasserthal and Hubrich of MFJ IV each downed a Camel near Deinze. That evening the German army counterattacked at Somerghem – a rare success after weeks of general retreat. MFJ IV scored again on 4 November, with Hubrich downing Camels south of Deinze and near Ghent, while Bühl was credited with a Dolphin south of Scheldewindeke for his sixth, and last, victory. Two No 204 Sqn Camels were lost, with Lt J R Chisman force landing in Allied lines unhurt. 2Lt John Lightbody, who had recently made ace with his fifth victory, was killed, however.

These were the last victories credited to the *Marine Feld Jastas* before a collapsing army, mutinies in the High Seas Fleet and Kaiser Wilhelm II's abdication led to Germany agreeing to an armistice on 11 November. World War 1 was officially over, but for several of the naval aces there was still some fighting ahead.

POST-WAR EXPLOITS

In addition to the *Pour le Mérite* and the Iron Cross 2nd Class, Gotthard Sachsenberg had received the House Order of Albert the Bear, Knight 1st Class with Sword, Friedrich Cross of Anhalt 1st and 2nd Classes,

Friedrich-August Cross of Oldenburg 1st and 2nd Classes and the Hanseatic Cross of Hamburg during the course of his wartime career. After the armistice, fighting broke out within Germany between communist elements such as the Sparticists and conservative volunteer militias, including the *Freikorps*.

Another challenge to post-war Germany attended the breakaway from Russia of Lithuania, Latvia and Estonia. When a border conflict commenced between the German republic and Lithuania, the Lithuania IV Reservekorps was mobilised in January 1919 under Generalmajor Rüdiger *Graf* von der Goltz. To provide air support, Sachsenberg formed the *Flieger Abteilung Ost* (dubbed *Kampfgruppe* Sachsenberg) consisting of 15 Junkers D Is, 15 Junkers CL Is, two Rumpler C IVs and a few Fokker D VIIs. Among the veterans who flew in the unit were Hans Goerth, Gerhard Hubrich, Karl Scharon, Alexander Zenses and Theo Osterkamp, as well as 48-victory *Luftstreistskräfte* ace Josef Jacobs.

Little aerial opposition was encountered, leaving the unit to perform ground attack missions in support of operations from Mitau to Riga until 16 November 1919, when it was ordered to withdraw. One thing that impressed Sachsenberg during the campaign was the durability of the all-metal Junkers monoplanes, which he rightly recognised as the aeroplanes of the future.

Following the end of hostilities Karl Scharon died on 26 May 1921. Reinhold Poss pursued an aviation career, but was killed on 26 August 1933 when he accidentally flew into a church steeple in Hagenow. Willy Thöne became an engineer and director with German civil aviation, eventually passing away in Mülheim-Ruhr on 17 January 1974. 'Küken' Hubrich flew airliners and then became a test pilot, extending the latter role into military aircraft when he joined the Luftwaffe in 1932. During World War 2 he rose to the rank of major and was alleged to have downed two Allied aircraft. He retained an interest in aviation until his death on 20 October 1972.

During the interwar years Gotthard Sachsenberg founded the airline Aero Lloyd, and later, in concert with Hannes von Schertel, established a firm in Dessau for designing and producing hydrofoils for boats and

Orden Pour le Mérite **recipients Josef Jacobs, Gotthard Sachsenberg and Theo Osterkamp pose for a post-war photograph alongside a Stöwer automobile prior to setting off for the Baltic to battle Lithuanians with Sachsenberg's** *Flieger Abteilung Ost* **in 1919 (***Greg VanWyngarden***)**

Commanding JG 51 in the opening months of World War 2, Theo Osterkamp added anything from two to six Allied aeroplanes to the 32 victories he had scored in the previous conflict (*Greg VanWyngarden*)

ships. A staunch anti-Nazi, he sat out World War 2, but a nephew, Ltn Heinz Sachsenberg, became a prominent Luftwaffe fighter pilot, chalking up 104 victories and receiving the *Ritterkreuz* while serving with *Jagdgeschwaderen* 52 and 7, as well as the Fw 190D-equipped protection flight for *Jagdverband* 44. Having survived the conflict, Sachsenberg died of complications from war wounds on 17 June 1951.

The hydrofoil plant established by Sachsenberg and von Schertel in Dessau was overrun by Soviet forces in 1945, but he re-established the firm in Switzerland as Supramar in 1953. Sachsenberg died of a heart attack in Bremen on 23 August 1961.

Edging out Sachsenberg as Germany's highest scoring naval ace of World War 1 with 32 victories, Theo Osterkamp received the *Pour le Mérite*, Iron Cross 1st and 2nd Classes and Knight's Cross of the Hohenzollern House Order. After taking part in fighting in the Baltic area in 1919, he joined the Luftwaffe in 1935 and commanded *Jagdfliegerschule* Nr I in 1939. On 19 September 1939, Osterkamp was given command of Bf 109E-equipped *Jagdgeschwader* 51.

During the German invasion of the Netherlands, 'Onkel Theo', as his men affectionately called him, made it clear that he was of no mind to administer the wing from behind a desk, and he duly shot down a Fokker G I over Soesterberg on 12 May 1940. Ten days later he downed an RAF Hurricane of No 605 Sqn over Roubaix, followed by another Hurricane over Dunkirk on 31 May and a Bristol Blenheim of No 107 Sqn on 1 June. Following the fall of France, Osterkamp was credited with a Spitfire off Dover on 13 July, although his victim was probably a Hurricane of No 56 Sqn. This gave Osterkamp the rare distinction of having become an ace in two wars, although there has been some dispute over the validity of his second, third and fourth victories. Osterkamp's aggressive leadership of JG 51 got him a promotion to generalmajor, but it also brought an unwelcome teletype from Berlin on 23 July;

'Hauptmann Mölders is to take over the wing, effective immediately. Generalmajor Osterkamp is to place himself at the disposal of *Luftflotte* 2.'

On 27 July Osterkamp briefed Major Werner Mölders, a 14-victory Spanish Civil War veteran of the *Legion Condor*, on how the situation had changed since he had last fought over France – Mölders had been a PoW during the latter stages of the Battle of France. That advice was reiterated to him the hard way when he led JG 51 over the Channel the following day, encountered RAF fighters and ended up belly landing in France with wounds that put him in hospital for the next ten days.

Osterkamp used this reprieve to fly combat missions for a bit longer, but he was ultimately withdrawn to receive the *Ritterkreuz des Eisernes Kreuzes* on 22 August and then command *Luftflotte* 2's fighter force on the Channel front until 1 August 1942, when he was transferred to North Africa. Osterkamp commanded all Luftwaffe fighter units on Sicily from 5 April to 15 June 1943, when he was replaced by Adolf Galland. From then on Osterkamp served in various staff and training positions, rising to the rank of Generalleutnant before being retired on 21 December 1944, partly because of his outspoken criticisms of High Command. Theo Osterkamp wrote a memoir, *Du Oder Ich: Jagdflieger in Höhen und Tiefen*. He died in Baden-Baden on 2 January 1975.

DETACHED DUTY

In addition to the *Marine Feld Jasta* aces, two German naval pilots achieved similar distinction while on detached duty with *Jagdstaffeln* of the *Luftstreitskräfte*.

Born in Munster on 16 January 1894, Konrad Mettlich began his military career flying Eindeckers with the Fokker *Staffel* attached to the 17. *Armee* in 1916. He then transferred to the navy, and in November of that year he was assigned to MFFA II. Flying alongside Ltn z S Gotthard Sachsenberg, Oblt z S Mettlich honed his aerial fighting skills and went on to become an original member of MFJ I in February 1917. Early in June, however, he was posted to army unit *Jagdstaffel* 8 and his career dramatically took wing.

On 8 June, shortly after his arrival at *Jasta* 8's aerodrome at Rumbeke, Mettlich engaged in a dogfight in which Oblt Bruno von Voigt downed Nieuport B1644 of No 1 Sqn west of Dadizeele at 1415 hrs, resulting in 2Lt R S L Boote being taken prisoner. Five minutes later Mettlich shot down two Pups of No 66 Sqn over Moorslede, killing 2Lt A G Robertson in A6207 and 2Lt A V Shirley in B1745.

On 28 July *Jasta* 8's CO, Hptm Gustav Stenzel, was killed in action near Rumbeke – he was probably flying the Albatros shot down in flames east of Roulers by 2Lt Thomas C Luke of No 66 Sqn. The next day, Oblt z S Mettlich was put in acting charge of the *Staffel*, leading it and handling administrative affairs until 9 August, when Hptm Constantin von Bentheim arrived to take permanent command. Three days later Mettlich resumed his scoring with another double. His first success was a British balloon of the 23rd Kite Balloon Section, 8th Company, 5th Wing (23-8-5), burned northwest of Vlamertighe at 1730 hrs. Mettlich's claim coincided with an identical one made by Ltn Xaver Dannhuber of *Jasta* 26, suggesting that the two German pilots attacked the balloon from different angles at the same time. Mettlich also brought down a Sopwith two-seater north of Ypres moments later.

While engaging Bristol Fighters on 9 September, *Jasta* 8's Ltn d R Rudolf Wendelmuth was credited with an F 2B destroyed southwest of Langemarck and Mettlich claimed a second example north of Zillebeke that was not confirmed. During a dogfight over Kruisstraat at 1230 hrs on the 23rd, however, Mettlich was credited with a Sopwith, bringing his tally to five, while Wendelmuth got another and Vfw Werner Seitz claimed a Nieuport near St Jean. Their opponents may have been from

Members of *Jagdstaffel* 8, including several naval personnel, in April 1917. Identified from left, standing, are Ltn Hans Körner (third), Offstv Walter Goettsch (fourth), Hptm Gustav Stenzel, CO, (sixth), Ltn Alfred Ulmer (seventh) and Vfw Wilhelm Seitz (eighth). In the top row are Oblt Rudolf *Freiherr* von Esebeck (first) and Hptm Hans von Hünerbein (second), while in the middle row at right in the darker uniform is Oblt z S Konrad Mettlich. After Stenzel's death on 28 July, Mettlich temporarily served as acting commander (*Greg VanWyngarden*)

Members of *Jasta* 7 at Thouroube aerodrome, near Roulers, in the summer of 1917. They are, from left to right (in the front row), Lt d R Carl Degelow, Ltn Wilhelm Nebgen, Uffz Jupp Böhne, unidentified British PoW, Obflmstr Kurt Schönfelder (with the cigarette in his mouth) and an unidentified pilot. '*Wassermann*' Schönfelder, a naval pilot attached to the *Staffel* to gain experience, became its second ranking ace after Ltn Josef Jacobs (*Carl Degelow via Peter Kilduff*)

'Naval 10', which engaged five two-seaters and ten escorting fighters near Westroosebeke and, in spite of frequent gun stoppages, credited an Albatros out of control each to Flt Cdrs Howard J T Saint and H Melville Alexander and Flt Sub-Lt Edward I Bussell. The latter pilot's aeroplane was badly shot up and he crashed, although Bussell was unhurt. Squadronmate Flt Sub-Lt Rowan H Day had to land at 'Naval 4's' aerodrome following this action.

Over the winter *Jasta* 8 moved thrice before settling at Wassigny in the 18. *Armee* sector in anticipation of the coming spring offensive. Mettlich did not score again until 12 March 1918, when he downed an SE 5a over Villevèque. The pilot, 2Lt P J Nolan of No 24 Sqn, forced landed in Allied lines uninjured.

At 1010 hrs the next day *Jasta* 8 had another scrap with SE 5as, this time from No 84 Sqn northeast of St Quentin. Things went badly for the Germans as Capt Frederick E Brown sent an Albatros crashing at Homblières and 2Lt Percy K Hobson's gunfire caused both sets of his adversary's wings to break away. Brown's opponent, Vfw Adolf Besenmüller, suffered severe stomach wounds, from which he died at Lesdins the next day. Hobson's victim was Oblt z S Mettlich, who crashed to his death at Remaucourt.

While little is known of Konrad Mettlich besides his deeds, fellow *Marine Feld* ace Kurt Schönfelder is mentioned in the memoirs of his commander, Josef Jacobs. Born in Totschen on 30 July 1894, Schönfelder was, like Mettlich, a prewar flier, having obtained his licence on 27 December 1913. Joining the navy, he had attained the rank of Oberflugmaat, or chief petty officer, by 23 August 1916, when he transferred to *Jasta* 7 to gain experience that he would hopefully impart to a naval fighter unit. Schönfelder would remain with the *Jasta*, however.

After making several unconfirmed claims in March and May 1917, Schönfelder officially opened his account on 20 July when he shot down an SE 5a over Passchendaele. Its pilot turned out to be Lt Robert G Jardine, a Canadian member of the formidable No 56 Sqn. His next success, a SPAD VII brought down intact northeast of Ypres on 16 August, was from another famous unit, *escadrille* N3. Its pilot, Sous-Lt Henri Rabatel with three victories, was wounded and taken prisoner.

On 18 October *Wassermann* ('water-bearer'), as *Jasta* 7's CO, Ltn Josef Jacobs, affectionately called Schönfelder, downed an F 2B. Jacobs, himself victor over a DH 4 that morning, logged the kill with grim terseness – 'Obflm Schönfelder, a Brisfit out of a squadron of five. The Englishman disintegrated'. His victim was one of three Bristols lost that day by No 22 Sqn, possibly A7125 in which 2Lts B B Perry and C H Bartlett went missing over Ardoye.

Now a trusted *Staffel* stalwart, Schönfelder started off 1918 by forcing a DH 4 of No 57 Sqn down near Courtrai on 26 February, its crew of

2Lt J M Allen and Capt F R Sutcliffe being taken prisoner. His next claim, a Nieuport west of Rumbeke on 6 March, came down in British lines and went unconfirmed – rightly, as it turned out, since *Jasta 7*'s opponents in No 40 Sqn suffered no casualties that day. He was credited with a Camel near Dickebusch on 16 May, although again British records shows no corresponding loss.

On 28 May Jacobs reported;

'We jumped five SE 5s who were tangling with a formation of Albatros D Vs. While attempting to beat down one of the enemy aircraft, I saw one of my own patrol in great difficulties so I went to his assistance. It turned out to be Uffz Sicho, who had been shot up by an SE 5 and was wounded in the arm and upper leg. He was able to land his ship smoothly at the airfield. Schönfelder and Sowa each gained victories.'

In addition to Sicho, Uffz Peisker was wounded. Vzfw Otto Sowa, a former *Jasta 7* man who had transferred to the newly formed *Jasta 52* on 9 January 1918, was credited with an SE 5a, as was his commander, Ltn Paul Billik. Their opponents were apparently from No 64 Sqn, which lost Lt William P Southall, killed by Billik, and No 84 Sqn, whose Capt Hugh W L Saunders claimed an enemy scout out of control, while Lt Roy Manzer collided with an attacking Albatros. This immediately threw his SE 5a upside down. After recovering, Manzer reported seeing the German scout going down minus its right wings.

On 31 May Jacobs' report included 'Obflm Schönfelder shot down a Camel in flames at the Forest of Nieppe'. Uffz August Eigenbrodt was also credited with a Camel in that action, but the identity of these aeroplanes remains uncertain.

Schönfelder started June off by bringing down a Camel of No 4 Sqn Australian Flying Corps (AFC) near Laventie on the 1st. Its pilot, 2Lt A Rintoyl, became a PoW. He downed another Camel near Oudekapelle on the 2nd, but this time the wounded pilot, Lt W A Hunter of No 54 Sqn, came down on his own side of the lines.

Schönfelder's tenth victory was a French balloon burned at Wattines on 3 June. The observer, Lt Payen of the *78e Compagnie des Aérostiers*, was wounded but parachuted safely to earth. Schönfelder gave a repeat performance for the British on 16 June when he destroyed a balloon of 47-11-1 northwest of Bethune. Later that day *Jasta 7* took on a number of SE 5as over the Brielen-Ypres road, two of which were claimed by Schönfelder and Ltn Willi Nebgen, but neither was confirmed.

Schönfelder poses alongside his Albatros D V in black *Jasta 7* livery, adorned with his golden star personal emblem. This marking also appeared on his Fokker D VII according to Ltn Jacobs, who wrote of Schönfelder 'He was one of the best pilots, being well known along the whole Western Front' (*Alex Imrie*)

At 0800 hrs on the morning of 18 June Camels of No 54 Sqn departed on a bombing raid, only to run afoul of *Jasta 7* over Armentières. In the ensuing scrap Schönfelder claimed a Camel between Ypres and Comines, and Camels were also credited to Uffz Max Mertens and Ltn Nebgen, for the loss of Ltn Max Hillmann, who was shot down in flames by

Schönfelder poses before his Fokker D VII with another RAF 'guest'. The latter, wearing an old RFC 'maternity jacket', may be 2Lt J Connelly of No 54 Sqn, who after being brought down by Schönfelder on 18 June 1918 was taken to Ste Marguerite to meet his vanquisher. The latter then gave him a 'guided tour' of the aerodrome, before having him join his captors at dinner (*HAC/UTD*)

Lt M Burger. Only one No 54 Sqn Camel was actually brought down. After a forced landing near the Ypres–Comines railway, 2Lt J Connelly was taken to Ste Marguerite to meet his opponent. Schönfelder duly took him on a guided tour of the aerodrome and its aeroplanes, after which Connelly joined his captors at dinner.

Jasta 7 suffered another loss the following day when Eigenbrodt and Mertens attacked two British balloons near Hazebrouck. Mertens sent one down smoking at Poperinghe, but as he went after the gasbag at Bailleul his Pfalz D IIIa was jumped by Capt Arthur H Cobby of No 4 Sqn AFC, who sent him crashing to his death in the Nieppe forest.

On the afternoon of 21 June a Camel of No 210 Sqn attacked Ltn Jacobs, who described what ensued;

'I was in combat for 28 minutes with a Camel who finally desisted and went after Obflm Schönfelder, whereupon I continued to rake him whenever I could find him in my sights. Eventually, Schönfelder forced the Camel down intact near Menin, and the pilot, a lieutenant, was made our prisoner. He related to us that it was his intention to add both Schönfelder and I to his rapidly increasing score, but, to the contrary, he was added as a victory to *Jagdstaffel* 7's list'.

Schönefelder's 13th victim, 19-year-old 2Lt R G Carr, had in fact only flown two previous patrols since arriving at No 210 Sqn on 13 June. Certainly not lacking in audacity, he escaped from his German captors on 1 July.

On 26 June Jacobs, in his black Fokker Dr I triplane, was leading a patrol of newly delivered Fokker D VIIs when they spotted 15 to 20 British aircraft dropping bombs near Ypres. 'We manoeuvred for position', he wrote, 'gaining some altitude, but were immediately jumped by three Sopwith Camels. I blazed away at one of them, who was slowly spiralling down, when I saw a Fokker D VII drop by me with his top right wing disintegrated. I recognised the golden star on the black fuselage of the Fokker. Seeing that Schönfelder's aircraft was totally disabled, I had to resume combat with my adversary, who was now in a steep dive toward Menin.

'As he attempted to straighten out, several times I jabbed away with both guns until the wings of the Camel folded up and the wreckage crashed into the ground at the Castle Park in Menin. When I later visited the wreckage there were only a few fragments, and, next to it, lay the dead body of Lt Boothman, who was 19 years old and belonged to No 210 Sqn, RAF. He had fought very courageously. This Camel was my 22nd victory.

'Upon arriving back at the base, I learned that Schönfelder had fallen near Bousbecque, and that his machine – a complete wreck – had hit a house'.

Jacobs' victim, Lt C D Boothman (in Camel D9614), was only on his fourth patrol since joining his unit on 10 June. Falling 15,000 ft to die just a few kilometres away, Schönfelder was probably flying the Fokker that was jointly credited to No 210 Sqn aces Capt Lawrence P Coombes and Lts Ian C Sanderson and Kenneth R Unger.

On 29 June *Jasta* 7's naval ace was buried with full honours in the cemetery at Linselles. 'May he rest in peace', said Jacobs during Schönfelder's ceremony. 'His *Staffel* will always keep him in faithful memory'.

ACES OVER THE BALTIC

Russian naval airmen often made aggressive use of the versatile flying boats that had been designed by Dmitry Pavlovich Grigorovich since 1913, in particular the Shchetinin M-9, which first flew on 9 January 1916.

The M-9's most successful pilot, Aleksandr Nikolayevich Prokofiev de Seversky, was born in Tiflis, Georgia, on 7 June 1894. Encouraged by his father, Nikolai P de Seversky, who was a leading member of the Imperial All-Russian Aero Club, Aleksandr learned to fly in 1908, prior to entering the Imperial Naval Academy in St Petersburg. In June 1915 he was assigned to the 2nd Bombing and Reconnaisance Squadron of the Baltic Fleet, based at Kilkond on Oesel Island.

On the evening of 15 July Lt Seversky's commander, Sqn Ldr Vladimir Litvinov, entered the officers' mess to announce that two German gunboats had been reported in a cove in the Gulf of Riga, and that all but one of the nearest Russian destroyers were otherwise occupied. He then asked for a volunteer to accompany him in an attempt to drive off the Germans using the four 20-lb bombs that each of their Lebedev-built FBA flying boats carried. 'I was a tough-muscled youngster with a daredevil streak', Seversky wrote later, and 'jumped to my feet faster than anyone else'.

Soon after takeoff from Kilkond Bay, high winds and heavy clouds caused Litvinov to abort the nocturnal mission. Neither Seversky nor his observer, Sgt Anatoly Blinov, saw Litvinov's hand gestures in the dim light, however, and they pressed on to attack one of the gunboats through a fusillade of cannon and small arms fire. The Russians managed to release all but one of their bombs, and Seversky saw one flash, suggesting a hit.

As the bullet-riddled FBA limped back to base, it splashed down hard and its remaining bomb exploded, killing Blinov and hurling Seversky into the bay. Rescued by a Russian destroyer, he was rushed to a clinic, where the doctors judged it necessary to amputate one of his legs below the knee. Later transferred to a hospital at Revel Naval Air Station (NAS), Seversky was visited by his father, who was then piloting Sikorsky Il'ya Muromets bombers in the frontline. Both rejected a doctor's recommendation for a further amputation at the hip. Aleksandr, who had briefly considered suicide, wanted as much flesh and bone as could be saved

Aleksandr Nikolayevich Prokofiev de Seversky undertook military flying training in a Farman MF 4 at Gatchina flight school in the spring of 1915 (*Jack Herris via Jon Guttman*)

Nikolai P de Seversky (right) visits his recuperating son in the hospital at St Petersburg in the autumn of 1915. (*Jack Herris via Jon Guttman*)

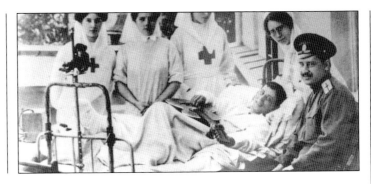

The most successful of Dmitry Grigorovich's flying boat designs was the two-seat M-9, which had a 150 hp Salmson radial engine that gave it a top speed of 68 mph. The aeroplane could be fitted with a Maxim (as shown here) or Lewis machine gun for the observer. No fewer than 500 examples were built by Shchetinin and deployed from 32 naval bases, as well as seaplane carriers. Both Russian naval aces, Aleksandr de Seversky and Mikhail Safanov, scored victories in M-9s (*Gennadiy Petrov archive via Carl Fredrik Geust*)

with the hope of fitting a prosthetic limb that would render him sufficiently fit to fly again.

Upon recovery, Seversky was made chief naval inspector for the Petrograd District in March 1916. During the course of his work he spent time with Dmitry Grigorovich at the Shchetinin Aircraft Company developing the M-9, emphasising the need for a forward rotating machine gun as well as thicker planking and some metal protection for the crew. Although its 120 hp Salmson radial engine gave it a maximum speed of only 68.3 mph (110 km/h), the M-9 had a range of 225 miles and could carry bombs as well as a Maxim, Hotchkiss or Lewis machine gun. It was even tested with a 20 mm Oerlikon or 37 mm Puteaux cannon. In the process of working with Grigorovich, Seversky acquired invaluable experience in aircraft design.

Meanwhile, Seversky had not only mastered his wooden leg, but on the pretext of ground testing aircraft he had learned how to work the rudder bar with it too. During a visit to Sebastopol in May, Seversky oversaw the assembly of new M-9s and then arranged an aerial demonstration, in which the flying boat dived, rolled and looped. The aerobatic display ended in gasps of disbelief when the audience of senior officers realised that Seversky had been the pilot. Seversky's superior, Capt M Shcherbachov, vowed to punish him for his unauthorised flight in direct defiance of standing orders, but others did not share his outrage. Rear Adm Adrian I Nepenin, commanding the Baltic Fleet, reported the incident to Tsar Nicholas II, praising Seversky's skill and daring, and broaching the question of allowing him to return to combat duty. The Tsar tersely replied, 'Read. Admire. Let Fly. Nikolai'.

On 1 July Seversky returned to Revel NAS in high style when he completed the first ferry flight of an M-9 to the base, instead of the flying boat having to be dismantled and transported there by lorry or train. He then rejoined the 2nd Bombing and Reconnaissance Detachment at Zerel, on Oesel Island.

Three days later, flying an M-9 from a new base at Runo Island, Seversky downed a

A close up of a Maxim machine gun mounted on a Shchetinin M-9. The circular housing at lower left held the wireless antenna (*Greg VanWyngarden*)

German Albatros C Ia (a C I two-seater converted into a seaplane) over the Gulf of Riga. After some reconnoitring, an M-9 crew pinpointed the base – at Lake Angern, near the Gulf of Riga's western shore – from where the Germans were operating their seaplanes. On 13 August three M-9s, flown by Lts Seversky, Diderichs and Steklov, set out to bomb the Lake Angern seaplane base. In spite of ground fire that hit all three flying boats, Seversky later claimed 'the naval base looked as if a cyclone had struck it'. Steklov's flying boat was hit in a radiator, but its second radiator delayed the engine's overheating and seizing up long enough for him to glide clear of the German coast, force land and be recovered by a Russian gunboat.

As Seversky and Diderichs turned away from the target, they were confronted by seven C Ias. Weaving in coordination with each other, the two Russian pilots fended off their opponents for an hour-and-three-quarters, driving down two of their attackers. When Diderichs' gun jammed, an Albatros closed in to finish his flying boat off, but Seversky put his M-9 on a collision course with the German and a close-range burst of fire from his observer sent it, too, nose-diving into the gulf. Shortly afterwards the appearance of more M-9s, which Seversky called 'the most beautiful sight I have ever seen', drove off the rest of the Germans, and he returned to Rudno with 30 bullet holes in his flying boat. As the first Russian credited with three victories in one mission, Seversky was promoted to senior lieutenant and awarded the Golden Sword of St George from the tsar himself.

As winter lessened combat operations, Seversky used the time to devise a universal ski mount for flying boats. In December he was reassigned to the Shchetinin factory as a technical advisor, monitoring the manufacture of his ski design, and its use on the new M-11 single-seat flying boat fighter.

In February 1917, with revolution leading to the establishment of a provisional government under Aleksandr Kerensky, de Seversky wished to steer clear of the political fervour in Petrograd. His request to return to the front was granted with command of the 2nd Naval Fighter Detachment, but before he could depart he suffered a freak accident, slipping beneath the wheel of a horse-drawn vehicle and breaking his other leg.

May saw Seversky employed as a technical advisor in Moscow, but in July he returned to the front to lead the fighter detachment on Oesel Island. While flying one of its Nieuport 21s on 10 October, he scored two more victories over Zerel Island. Four days later German warships bombarded the airfield, destroying it and compelling Seversky's unit to evacuate Oesel Island in the face of an amphibious invasion force. As the remaining aeroplanes flew off, engine trouble forced Seversky down in German-occupied territory. Removing the machine gun and several instruments from his aeroplane, he managed to walk ten miles and regain Russian lines. For this feat he was promoted to lieutenant commander and awarded the Order of St George 4th Class.

In March 1918 Seversky was sent to serve as assistant naval attaché to the United States, and as a result of the Bolshevik Revolution – which rendered an officer of his blue-blooded pedigree persona non grata – he would remain there, becoming a citizen in 1927 and embarking on a career as designer for the aircraft manufacturer bearing his name. Among Alexander Seversky's products were the BT-8 (the first all-metal monoplane trainer accepted for service by the US Army Air Corps in 1935), the P-35 (the USAAC's first all-metal cantilever construction stressed-skin monoplane fighter in 1936) and the P-43 (the USAAC's first fighter fitted with an air-cooled supercharged engine in 1938). In February 1939, however, he was voted off the board of his own company, which was subsequently reorganised as the Republic Aircraft Company. Seversky remained active in aviation until his death on 24 August 1974.

Russia's other naval ace also served with the Baltic Fleet, and like Seversky he too started out in flying boats. Born of noble blood in

Flying this Nieuport 21 while commanding a fighter detachment on Oesel Island on 10 October 1917, Seversky downed a German bomber and its fighter escort over Zerel, taking his tally to six victories (*Jack Herris via Jon Guttman*)

Ostrogozhk, in Voronezh province, on 13 November 1893, Mikhail Ivanovich Safanov entered the Imperial Naval Academy on 20 September 1909, graduating as a michman (warrant officer) in May 1914. During the early years of the war he served aboard the battleships *Gromoboi* and *Sevastopol*, before requesting a transfer to the aviation section of the Baltic Fleet, which was approved on 24 November 1915. He made his first solo flight on 1 December and completed his pilot training at the Revel NAS in March 1916. Days later he was assigned to the Baltic Fleet's 3rd NAS on the Gulf of Riga. There he flew Maurice Farman MF 11 flying boats.

In the summer of 1916 the Baltic Fleet reorganised its air arm into two divisions. On 11 August Safanov was assigned to the 1st Air Detachment 'Glagol' of the Second Air Division.

Sea and air activity in the sector was increasing, and several encounters took place on 9 September 1916, including one between five German and five Russian aeroplanes over the Mikhailovsky Lighthouse. Safanov's M-9 No 29 was hit four times during the engagement, suffering radiator damage, but he and his observer, Orlov, drove one of their opponents down to force land in the Irben River. Ten days after being credited with his first victory, Safanov was awarded the Order of St Anne 4th Class.

As Safanov, Orlov and a second M-9 crew flew a bombing sortie against the German base at Lake Angern on 26 September, they were intercepted by what they estimated to be 20 enemy aeroplanes. Safanov was severely wounded in the leg, and when the other M-9 tried to come to his aid it was shot down and its crew killed. In spite of the odds, Safanov managed to fight his way out and brought his observer home. In the following months his outstanding service earned him the Order of St Stanislaus 3rd Class with Swords and Ribbon and the Order of St Vladimir 4th Class, with Sword and Ribbon, as well as promotion to lieutenant on 10 July 1917.

Four days later Safanov was given command of the 'Glagol' air detachment. That same day he took off in an M-15 flying boat, accompanied by a second machine, to intercept a German aeroplane approaching Arensburg. Closing to 100 metres, Safanov fired and saw

A Shchetinin M-15 at Oranienbaum in 1919. A somewhat downsized version of the M-9, the M-15 was powered by a 150 hp Hispano-Suiza engine that gave it a maximum speed of 77.7 mph. Half of the 80 produced served as trainers, but Lt Mikhail I Safanov scored his second victory in one (*Gennadiy Petrov archive via Carl Fredrik Geust*)

Mikhail I Safanov and his wife, Ludmila Tscheboratoriova, beside the Nieuport 10 in which they escaped from Bolshevik-dominated Russia on 11 April 1918. It bears the blue and white insignia of the Finnish air arm, with which Safanov briefly flew under the pseudonym of Mikko Vuorenheimo (*Gennadiy Petrov archive via Carl Fredrik Geust*)

his foe lose altitude. Although nobody saw it crash, the aeroplane was credited as his second victory.

Safanov was flying a conventional Nieuport 21 sesquiplane (serial NR-1) during a dogfight on 7 September that involved five such fighters, and M-15 flying boats, against three German aeroplanes over Arensburg. Getting on the tail of a two-seater, he fired ten to fifteen rounds from a distance of 50 metres and later reported his quarry shot down. On 25 October Safanov was promoted to senior lieutenant and granted a short leave, during which time he married Ludmila Tscheboratoriova. Upon returning to the front on 14 November, Safanov took command of the 2nd Land Fighter Detachment at Kuiavtoin. Two days later German aircraft reconnoitred Moon Island and Safanov took off to intercept them in Nieuport 21 NR-1. At 0915 hrs he caught an intruder and sent it down to crash on Moon Island.

The next morning the Germans returned to bomb Russian warships that were moored at Moon Island, and at 0900 hrs Safanov and Nieuport 21 NR-1 were up again. This time he caught a twin-engined bomber, which he drove down smoking into the Gulf of Riga for his fifth victory.

Soon after that, the Bolshevik Revolution threw Russia into chaos, amid which Poland and Finland declared independence. Safanov and four other anti-Bolsehvik pilots flew to Finland, the ace taking off from Komendantsky airfield with his wife in a Nieuport 10 on 11 April 1918. After flying for the Finns, he returned to Russia to join Gen Anton Denikin's White Army near Novocherkassk. With the cause collapsing, he and his wife travelled through Persia to India, where he joined the RAF.

In 1924 Safanov, his wife and two children moved again, this time to China, to help organise a naval training school. However, while testing a new flying boat in May 1924, he fatally crashed in the Ming River. Some years later, Safanov's wife and children settled in the United States.

Safanov, seated second from left, among other volunteers in Finnish service, but still under government suspicion. In the summer of 1918 he obtained the papers to travel though German-occupied Russia to join Anton Denikin's White Army (*via Jack Herris*)

ACTION OVER THE ADRIATIC

Russia was not the only power to boast aces in flying boats. Such aeroplanes, in fact, attained a remarkable ubiquity over the Adriatic Sea, which after Italy's declaration of war against Austria-Hungary on 25 May 1915 became an intense combat arena. Ironically, Austria-Hungary produced a flying boat fighter – albeit an improvised one – before it had an indigenously designed land-based fighter.

The exceptional character behind that creation was born Godfrey Richard Banfield in Castelnuovo (now Boka Kotorska, in Montenegro) on 6 February 1890, and was of Irish ancestry. Indeed, he was a British subject until 1903, when he became an Austrian citizen and followed his father's career in the *Kaiserlische und Königlische Kriegsmarine*. The renamed Gottfried Banfield earned his pilot's certificate in August 1912, and the outbreak of war found him stationed at the Pola naval base. A month later, in June 1915, he helped establish a naval air station at Trieste. Located 70 miles from Venice, ten miles from the mouth of the Isonzo River, 60 miles from the Piave and just 18 miles from the Italian naval base at Grado, Trieste-based flying boat crews of the *Seeflugwesen* frequently supported army operations in Italy, as well as patrolling the Adriatic.

While overflying the mouth of the Isonzo in Lohner L47 on 27 June 1915, Frglt Banfield and his observer, Seekadett Herbert Strohl Edler von Ravelsburg, spotted an Italian kite balloon and destroyed it with 500 rounds. The balloon was credited as the future ace's first victory.

Banfield was given command of Trieste NAS in February 1916, and on 5 April he made his first flight in L16 – a Lohner Type M flying boat that he had modified into a single-seater through the bolting of a Schwarzlose

An Irishman who became an Austrian citizen in 1903, Godfrey Richard Banfield was the most successful flying boat ace of World War 1 as Lschlt Gottfried Banfield. (*Jon Guttman*)

Banfield stands before his Lohner Type M L16, modified into a single-seater and fitted with an 8 mm Schwarzlose 07/12 machine gun bolted atop the hull. He scored five victories in this machine, four of them in August 1916 (*Aaron Weaver*)

MG 07/12 machine gun to the hull in front of the cockpit. On 1 May Banfield was promoted to Linienschiffsleutnant (lieutenant commander).

On the evening of 23 June Banfield attacked a French FBA Type C flying boat over the Gulf of Trieste, fatally striking its Italian observer, 2º Capo Grammaticopoulo, in the head and heart. Landing, the French pilot, Enseigne de Vaisseau de 1e Classe André Victor Vaugeois, tried to taxi toward Grado, but Banfield's gunfire crippled his engine. Vaugeois then manned the observer's gun, and he fought on until 100 rounds from Banfield disabled the weapon and hit him in the neck. After Vaugeois' wound was seen to, Banfield invited him to dinner, where he toasted the Frenchman's tenacious courage. The recovered FBA was displayed in Vienna's War History Museum. The next day, Banfield sent another FBA crashing into the Gulf of Trieste. This time Italian motorboats arrived to tow the flying boat and its wounded crew back to Grado.

Banfield's next success occurred on 1 August when he intercepted a formation of Caproni Ca.1s en route to bomb Fiume naval base. He forced one of them to crash-land on the Volasca parade grounds, where the crew was taken prisoner. Five days later, Banfield, in L16, joined Lohner L99 in attacking a Caproni of *4ª Squadriglia Aeroplani* at 9000 ft over Miramare. A bullet struck L99's radiator, forcing its crew to glide back to Trieste, but Banfield shot out all three of the Ca.1's engines and it crashed into a house southeast of Sistiana. The pilot, Sottotenente Valentino Zannini, died, but his co-pilot, Sergente Mario Borghi, and observer, Sergente Biagio Manieri, emerged wounded but alive.

On the night of 9 August Banfield led 21 flying boats from Trieste and its substations at Puntisella, Cosada and Parenzo in a bombing raid on Venice, during which a bomb hit and sank the British submarine *B10*, and *B8* was damaged. Notwithstanding the fact that the former, having just returned from patrol, had been caught in harbour, this marked the first time in history that an aircraft had sunk a submarine.

On 15 August Banfield shot down two French-flown FBA Type Hs. The crew of the first flying boat to be downed was wounded, while the other's, Enseigne de Vaisseau Baron Jean Roulier (commander of all French navy flyers on the Isonzo front) and Méchanicien A H Cousterousse, was killed.

Banfield's month of success said much for the soundness of the Lohner flying boat. It also encouraged the development of small single-seaters such as the Brandenburg CC, whose biplane wing cellule was supported by the same 'star strut' arrangement as used in the firm's D I land-based fighter, and whose designation was simply the initials of Hansa-Brandenburg's owner, Camillo Castiglione.

Banfield flew a CC to claim an unconfirmed victory over an Italian Farman on 13 October

Banfield returns to Trieste in November 1916 after a test flight in the 185 hp Austro-Daimler-powered Hansa-Brandenburg CC, presented to him by the firm's financier – for whom its initials stand – Camillo Castiglioni. Flying CC A12 on 3 December, Banfield shared in bringing down a Caproni bomber over Mavinje for his eighth victory (*Greg VanWyngarden*)

1916. He was also in a CC (with the *Abwehr* number A12) when he shared in the destruction of a Caproni over Mavinje on 3 December with army pilots Oblt Godwin Brumowski of *Fliegerkompagnie* (*Flik*) 12 (in Brandenburg D I 65.53) and Zugsführer Karl Cislaghi of *Flik* 28 (in the prototype Aviatik D I).

Banfield's next confirmed victory did not occur until 1917, by which time both Austria-Hungary and Italy had introduced more flying boat fighters to their arsenals. Hansa-Brandenburg replaced the CC's star-strut arrangement with more conventional interplane struts and installed a more powerful 200-230 hp Hiero engine to produce the W 18. Josef Mickl also designed a unique single-seater specifically for Banfield, the Oeffag Type H, which received the *Abwehr* serial A11. Banfield painted the flying boat blue, explaining that 'it seemed to be a good colour for camouflage for flying over water. More than this, however, it seemed a very good colour for night flying, which I did a lot of in the "Blue Wonder"'.

Indeed, at 2330 hrs on 31 May 1917, Banfield used A11 to shoot down an Allied flying boat near the mouth of the Primero River. The Italians towed the downed aeroplane back to Grado the next morning. This was the first nocturnal victory by any Austro-Hungarian pilot, and Banfield's ninth success overall. He would make further claims thereafter, but none were confirmed.

Less is known of the *KuK Seeflugwesen's* other ace, Friedrich Lang. Born in Austria, he joined the navy in 1912 and was awarded the *Silber Tapferkeitmedaille* 2nd Class for service aboard the destroyer *Balaton*, prior to his entering the Naval Fliers' School on the isle of Cosada on 21 March 1916. On 1 May he was promoted to Fregattenleutnant and on 20 June he earned his pilot's certificate.

Designed by Josef Mickl specifically for Gottfried Banfield, the Oeffag Type H was powered by a 200 hp Hiero engine and mounted two Schwarzlose MG 07/12 machine guns (*Aaron Weaver*)

Banfield in the cockpit of the Oeffag Type H, which he had painted blue overall with the *Abwehr* serial A11 reapplied in black. In spite of his success with the flying boat, and his endorsement that it be put in production, it never was (*Aaron Weaver*)

After a brief stint at Kumbor, Lang was stationed at Durazzo (now Durrës, in Albania). On 22 August 1916, six Farman pushers of the Italian *34ª Squadriglia* left Piskupi on a bombing mission to Durazzo. The base learned of the threat, as did the army's *Flik* 6, based at Skutari. Zugsführer Julius Arigi violated an Austro-Hungarian army regulation against an NCO flying without an officer observer by taking off from Skutari to intercept them in his Brandenburg C I, with Fw Johann Lasi in the observer's pit. During the course of a 30-minute fight, Arigi and Lasi were credited with driving two of the Farmans into the Skumbi River and three others into the sea two miles offshore, where Italian motorboats rescued all the crewmen. Arigi went on to become the second-ranking Austro-Hungarian ace with 32 victories.

Lang, with Einjährig-Freiwilliger Stabsmaschinenwärter Franz Kohlhauser, in Lohner Type TL L131 also intercepted the enemy formation between Cape Laghi and the Skumbi River estuary. Lang closed to 150 yards and Kohlhauser engaged a Farman in a ten-minute exchange of gunfire until the Italians jettisoned their bombs and ditched near a destroyer, which rescued them.

Lang and Kohlhauser then sighted a second Farman, whose crew they stated wore French uniforms. After a bitter 30-minute gun duel, the Farman also force-landed beside an Italian destroyer, while the victorious Austrians brought their riddled Lohner home for extensive repairs. Exceptional though their deeds were, it seems that Lang and Kohlhauser duplicated some of Arigi's claims that day. Further muddying the waters are the Italian losses for the action, which totalled only two aeroplanes – Farman 1704, crewed by Sergente Schiona and Capitano Scarioni, and a second aeroplane crewed by Caporale Rosse and Tenente Viziano.

In January 1917 Lang was reassigned to Pola, 85 miles southeast of Venice. There, his service earned him the *Militärverdienstkreuz* 3rd Class with War Decoration with Swords and the *Silber Militärverdienstmedaille* with Swords.

As Italian air raids increased, Pola's air defences were augmented by a land-based fighter detachment at Altura airfield, just inland from the naval base. Flying Phönix D Is with that unit, Lang would subsequently achieve acedom in August 1918 fighting, among other adversaries, a formidable Italian flying boat scout.

Long before Gottfried Banfield got the idea of converting his L16 into a fighter, the Italians had been sufficiently impressed with Ludwig Lohner's flying boats to copy the design. When a broken engine shaft caused Lohner Type T flying boat L40 to fall into Italian hands near Volano on 27 May 1915 – just three days after war had been declared – the *Regia Marina* ordered the Macchi firm to build ten aeroplanes just like it. Although Macchi had no previous experience

Austria's other naval ace, Frgltn Friedrich Lang, scored his first two victories in a flying boat in what may have been a case of multiple claiming. His next three were credited in Phönix D I land-based fighters in defence of Pola naval base (*via Jack Herris*)

Operating from Durazzo, Lang was credited with his first two victories piloting UFAG-built Lohner TL L131, with Stabsmaschinenwärter Franz Kohlhauser as his observer, on 22 August 1916 under circumstances that suggest over or duplicate claiming with *Flik* 6's Brandenburg C I team of Zugsführer Julius Arigi and Fw Johann Lasi (*Aaron Weaver*)

Italy's leading naval ace, Tenente di Vascello Orazio Pierozzi was also an outstanding leader who believed in teamwork. He also used a gun camera to help the members of the two *squadriglie* (*260ª* and *261ª*) he led from Venice hone their aerial marksmanship (*Gregory Alegi*)

Licence-built FBA Type H No 407, bearing the SIAI trademark on its bow, lies dockside in front of the armoured cruiser *Pisa* in Brindisi harbour. While leading FBA-equipped *255ª Squadriglia* from this naval base, Tenente di Vascello Orazio Pierozzi, in concert with his observer, Ercole Berlingeri, scored his first victory on 7 June 1917 (*Paolo Varriale*)

in flying boats, technical co-director Carlo Felice Buzio and his staff managed to reverse-engineer the Type T to accept a 150 hp six-cylinder Isotta-Fraschini V4 engine. Entering production in September, the Macchi L.1 evolved into a successful series that included the single-seat M.5.

Tested in May 1917, the M.5 was essentially a downsized Lohner hull with a sesquiplane wing inspired by Nieuport land-based fighters, which Macchi also built under licence. Powered by a 190 hp Isotta-Fraschini V4B engine, it had a maximum speed of 117 mph, a ceiling of 20,340 ft and an endurance of 3 hours 40 minutes. That performance, combined with two 0.303-in Vickers machine guns mounted inside the hull, made the M.5 the best, and with 348 examples built, the most-produced flying boat fighter of the war.

The first unit to receive the M.5 was *260ª Squadriglia*, formed in Venice under the command of Tenente di Vascello Luigi Bologna in November 1917 and operating from Miraglia NAS at Sant'Andrea. In addition to its M.5s, the squadron had an M.7 and tested floatplane versions of the SVA and Hanriot HD 1. In early 1918 the unit was joined by *261ª Squadriglia*, led by Sottotenente di Vascello Domenico Arcidiacono.

Italy's most successful naval fighter pilot was Orazio Pierozzi, who was born in the Tuscan hill town of San Casciano Val di Pesa on 8 December 1889. His father, Gustavo, was a doctor who had been one of the '1000' volunteers who followed Giuseppe Garibaldi when he delivered the Kingdom of Naples to King Vittorio Emanuele II in 1860. In 1908 Pierozzi entered the Naval Academy at Livorno, and during one of the school's annual training cruises to New York he photographed a flight by Wilbur Wright. He served on warships after getting his commission in January 1914, but on 15 June 1916 he enrolled at the

military flying school of Sestro Calende, near Lake Maggiore. During a training flight Pierozzi recklessly banked his FBA beyond what his instructors had advised until it fell into a spin, but then showed his technical acumen as he calmly analysed the situation, throttled back his engine and left the controls free to correct themselves. The flying boat still crashed, breaking Pierozzi's leg, but he regarded what he had learned from the experience as all the more reason to continue flying.

On 16 October 1916 Tenente de Vascello Pierozzi was assigned to the Brindisi Seaplane Station. In the spring of 1917, Italian naval units were reorganised and Pierozzi was given command of Brindisi's new *255ᵃ Squadriglia*, equipped with 20 FBAs.

On 15 May the *KuK Kriegsmarine* launched a foray by three light cruisers and two destroyers, commanded by Konteradmiral Miklos Horthy, against the Allied barrage of drifters lined across the Adriatic to blockade enemy submarine traffic. A day of fighting ended with the Austro-Hungarians sinking two Italian destroyers, two merchant ships and dozens of drifters. Amid the battle, Pierozzi, with Sottotenente di Vascello Luigi Lombardi di Lomborgo, and another FBA crew near-missed the cruisers *Saida*, *Novara* and *Helgoland* with bombs, then tangled with two UFAG-built Hansa-Brandenburg FBU flying boats that had been strafing Allied ships. K179, crewed by Frglt Otto *Freiherr* von Klimberg and Heinrich Schramek, was hit ten times, but their return fire forced Pierozzi to land in the sea between the two fleets, whose salvo exchanges further damaged his flying boat. After saving the machine guns, Pierozzi and Lombardi scuttled the FBA and were rescued by the French destroyer *Bisson*.

On 7 June the Italian anti-submarine airship *DE 5* was attacked by three Brandenburg K-boats, which put 30 bullets into it. Responding to the attack, Pierozzi took off with gunner Ercole Bellingeri in FBA No 14, joined by a Macchi L.3. They caught up with K154, whose crewmen may initially have mistaken them for their two wingmen, and in the ensuing fight the L.3's wing struck the K-boat hull. A burst from Bellingeri's gun hit the crew and sent K154 crashing into the sea, killing Linienschiffsleutnant Alois Poljanek and Stabsbootmann Prauer. Meanwhile, the L.3 had also crashed, and Pierozzi landed nearby to rescue the observer, Sottotenente di Vacello Carlo Daviso di Charvensod. Repeated dives could not locate the pilot, however – his body was recovered later, with a bullet in the forehead.

Raid and counter-raid continued, during which *255ᵃ Squadriglia* received more L.3s, new Macchi M.5 fighters and a Blackburn-built Sopwith Baby seaplane that Pierozzi enjoyed flying. Then, on 18 March 1918, he was reassigned to Venice to lead the new 'Gruppo Idrocaccia Venezia', comprised of *260ᵃ* and *261ᵃ squadriglie*.

Although short in stature, Pierozzi proved to be a good leader, an able trainer and a keen student of whatever was new. He was also a zealous advocate of formation flying, and teamwork over individualism. When, during a visit to Venice, King Vittorio Emanuele III asked Pierozzi

Pierozzi sits in the cockpit of M.5 M7256, with which he led the flying boat fighters of *Stazione Idrovolanti di Venezia*, scoring six of his seven victories in the process. Besides *361ᵃ Squadriglia's* white sawtooth pattern to the hull undersurfaces, the flying boat was also adorned with artwork of a hunting dog holding a broken Austrian flying boat in its jaws (*Roberto Gentilli*)

which pilot had brought down an Austrian flying boat fighter intact, he answered, 'The whole squadron, Your Majesty'.

Pierozzi led his first escort mission from Venice on 13 April, followed by four more that month. On the 22nd M.5s of *260ª Squadriglia* were escorting bombers attempting to target the battleship *Tegetthoff*, off Fasana, when the Italians spotted an enemy flying boat conducting an anti-submarine patrol. They attacked, joined by an L.3 of *251ª Squadriglia*, and after a 15-minute fight Lohner TL flying

Guardia Marina Umberto Calvello (right) and two of his mechanics pose before his M.5 M7289 of *260ª Squadriglia*, bearing the number 2 and a variation on the popular Italian cartoon character *Fortunello*, itself based on Frederick Burr Opper's comic strip *The Happy Hooligan* (*Paolo Varriale*)

boat R1 was shot down. Its crew, Machinenmaat Stefan Bauer and Seefähnrich Alfred Edler von Herbetz, were rescued by torpedo boat *Tb 88*. An L.3 was also shot down by Fähnrich Ernst Strecker in Brandenburg W 18 A59, and its crew rescued by *Tb 88* too, whereupon they became PoWs. The M.5 pilots sharing in R1's demise were Sottotenente di Vascello Umberto Calvello, 2i Capo Andrea Rivieri and Marinaiò (Seaman) Giuseppe Pagliacci.

Born in Pistoia, Tuscany, on 28 May 1897, Calvello came from a Neopolitan family with strong military traditions. Indeed, he had a former general for a father, who gave him a disciplined upbringing. In July 1916 Umberto enlisted in the *Regia Marina*. Initially serving as an observer in *251ª Squadrigia* in Venice, he earned a *Medaglia de Bronzo* for 'daring and exemplary prowess' during a raid on Trieste on the night of 30 June 1917.

Later in the summer of 1917, Calvello reported for pilot training, completing his first solo flight on 10 September and earning his brevet on the 26th. He flew his first combat sortie, over the Tagliamento River, on the 30th. After taking part in five reconnaissance missions in October and 13 bombing missions in November, Calvello converted onto the M.5 fighter in December and was transferred to *260ª Squadriglia*, then commanded by Ten di Vasc Federico Martinengo.

Born in Rome on 18 July 1897, Federico Carlo Martinengo had entered the *Reggia Accademia Navale* at Livorno in September 1911. Serving aboard the battleship *Dante Alleghieri*, he received his commission on 24 May 1915 – the day after Italy entered the war. Responding to his country's acute need for airmen, he entered the aviation school at Taranto on 27 December, training on Curtiss flying boats.

Assigned to the *Stazione Idrovolante* in Venice on 16 September 1916, Sottotenente di Vascello Martinengo first saw action on 16 October when he was an observer aboard FBA No 408 that had been sent to bomb Pola – onc of three flying boats despatched. An FBA dropped out with engine trouble and the remaining two flying boats became separated in bad weather. Spotting three Austro-Hungarian torpedo boats through a break in the haze, Martinengo, deciding that it was impossible to reach

Tenente di Vascello Federico C Martinengo commanded *260ª Squadriglia* at Sant' Andrea from December 1917 to June 1918, during which time he was credited with five victories. His *Medaglia d'Oro al Valore Militare*, however, was awarded posthumously for heroism in World War 2 (*Paolo Varriale*)

Pola, signalled his pilot, 2º Capo Pietro Valdimiro, to attack the vessels. Martinengo dropped the FBA's four bombs, and moments later the aeroplane was attacked by an enemy flying boat. Valdimiro manoeuvred his machine around, above and behind their foe, allowing Martinengo to hit it with an accurate burst of machine gun fire. The Italians saw their opponent glide down, its engine stopped.

Martinengo ordered another attack on the ships, but two more Austrian flying boats intervened. When the Italians ran out of ammunition they had to disengage and seek cover in the clouds. They were still 25 miles from home when their engine failed, but torpedo boat *15 OS* was nearby and it towed the FBA back to Venice. The Italians were credited with the enemy flying boat destroyed, but both it and its crewmen were evidently rescued by their own torpedo boats.

On 23 October Austro-Hungarian aeroplanes attacked Caorle. They were intercepted en route by Macchi L.2 LC 252, crewed by 2º Capo Daniele Minciotti and Martinengo (again in the observer's pit), as well as Nieuport land-based fighters of French *escadrille* N392, which had been assigned to help defend Venice. During the course of the fight Minciotti, Martinengo and Sous-Lt Paul Xavier Garros of N392 brought down Lohner L138, which was captured, along with its pilot, Seekadett Ferenc Viranyi, although the observer, E F Hoch, was killed.

On 11 November Martinengo was given command of *1ª Squadrigia* at Grado. There, he established a reputation as a superb organiser, as well as an open, affable leader of men. On 5 August 1917 Martinengo passed command of the unit, which had been redesignated *253ª Squadriglia*, to senior officer Ten di Vasc Aldo Pellegrini, although he remained with the squadron. On the 20th he had his first flight in the Macchi M.5.

Martinengo was reassigned to *260ª Squadriglia* on 28 October, and eight days later the new fighter unit flew its first combat sortie. This proved to be a disaster. As Martenengo and Guardiamarina Paolo Morterra escorted an L.3 of *259ª Squadriglia* on a bombing run on an enemy pontoon bridge near Latisana, they were bounced by three Oeffag-Albatros D IIIs of *Fliegerkompagnie* 41/J. The M.5s' best efforts could not prevent the L.3's destruction in flames, and the death of its crew, Tenenti di Vascello Arnaldo di Filippis – CO of the *259ª Squadriglia* – and Francesco Cappa.

In his doleful combat report Martinengo noted that the lead enemy fighter was painted bright red overall, and indeed the kill was jointly credited to three aces, Hptms Godwin Brumowski (who flew the all-red Albatros with skulls on the fuselage) and Frank Linke-Crawford and Oblt Rudolf Szepessy-Szekell *Freiherr* von Negyes és Renö. The day after scoring his fifth victory, however, Szepessy-Szekell was shot down and killed by Maggiore Francesco Baracca and Tenente Giuliano Parvis of *91ª Squadriglia*.

In December Martinengo was given command of *260ª Squadriglia* and on 21 February 1918 he was promoted to tenente di vascello.

On 1 May Tenente de Vascello Pierozzi claimed his first success since being given command of *261ª Squadriglia*. Leading a formation of three M.5s charged with escorting an L.3 on a photo-reconnaissance mission to Trieste, he spotted an enemy seaplane over Grado on the return leg of the flight and dived to attack it. With the other Macchis cutting off his

Three of Calvello's five victories were shared – with Martinengo among others – on 4 May 1918. One was Hansa-Brandenburg W 18 A78, shown here being towed through Venice to Sant' Andrea by a small motor boat. The pilot, Flgst Ferenc Börös, was taken prisoner (*Paolo Varriale*)

escape route, the pilot of Brandenburg W 18 A67, Fähnrich in der Reserve Josef Niedermeyer, put a few rounds into Pierozzi's flying boat before the Italian set his engine on fire, forcing him to land.

Niedermeyer managed to evade capture, and on 4 May he was up again in A91, along with three other W 18 pilots, to challenge an L.3 on a photo-reconnaissance mission over Punta Salvore. Pierozzi again led its five-flying boat escort, but made no claims in the ensuing melée, although his comrades were credited with three victories. One of the latter was Niedermeyer, who this time was captured by a nearby Italian torpedo boat.

Descending to investigate Niedermeyer's plight, Flgst Ferenc Börös spotted an Italian flying boat circling over the downed W 18 A91 and

Brandenburg W 18 A91, also brought down on 4 May 1918, displays hull damage from the 0.303-in Vickers guns of several M.5s. Its pilot, Ltn Josef Niedermeyer, had been downed three days earlier by Pierozzi and other members of *261ª Squadriglia*. He had returned to Trieste on that occasion, but this time he was captured. A third W 18, A82, was also driven down, but its pilot, Lschlt Gottfried Banfield, landed in Austrian waters (*Paolo Varriale*)

attacked, but failed to 'watch his six' and suddenly had four more Macchis on his tail. Struck several times, Böros' engine lost fuel pressure and he too alit in the sea, where he and his W 18, A78, were also captured.

Towed back to Sant' Andrea, the two Brandenburgs were jointly credited to Cavello, Martinengo, 2i Capi Andrea Rivieri, Giuseppe Pagliacci and Marinaió Guido Jannello. They were also credited with a third victory, but damaged W 18 A82 came down in friendlier waters and returned to Trieste. From the Italian standpoint it was truly the 'one that got away', for its lucky pilot was none other than Lschlt Gottfried Banfield.

The day's fight brought Martinengo's victory tally to five – and none too soon. On 8 June, with two years and 172 combat missions in his logbook, he was reassigned to serve as Director of Special Courses (i.e. fighter training) at the flying school at Lake Bolsena. On 14 September he was transferred to command the *Stazione Idrovolanti* at Otronto.

Although details of Calvello's alleged fifth victory have yet to be found, Italy officially regards him as an ace. Pierozzi's score then stood at two, but that was about to change.

On 14 May the experimental tracked torpedo vessel *Grillo*, crewed by Capitano Mario Pellegrini, made an unsuccessful attempt to crawl over the anti-submarine nets protecting Pola harbour and attack the battleship *Viribus Unitis*. Italian warships covering the operation came under attack from two Lohner bombers escorted by four W 18s, but these in turn were jumped by Pierozzi, who was leading a formation of five M.5s from *261ª Squadriglia*. The K-boats hastily dropped their bombs and fled, and in the subsequent clash of fighters the Italians again claimed three victories, although the Austrians only recorded two losses. Hit in the engine, W 18 A70 force landed in the sea, where Flgmt Josef Gindl was rescued and his disabled flying boat destroyed by *Tb 80*. Pierozzi also shot down A85, killing Seekadett Franz Pichl. Later obtaining a photograph of his victim, Pierozzi preserved it in his album, marked with words of sorrow and respect for his late adversary.

On 19 May four of *261ª Squadriglia's* Macchis were escorting two reconnaissance aeroplanes to Pola when they were intercepted by four Phönix D Is, led by Frglt Lang in A115. The Austrians were credited with downing two of the M.5s 20 miles east of the mouth of the Po River, but the Italians recorded only one loss. M.5 7280 No 14, flown by Ten di Vasc Umberto Magaldi, was found drifting 17 miles

These Phönix D Is were assigned to the defence flight stationed at Altura airfield near Pola, which Frglt Lang led throughout 1918. He was credited with his last three victories flying Phönix D Is, although he and his pilots sometimes found the M.5 to be a formidable adversary (*via Aaron Weaver*)

west of Rovigno by *Tb 81*, which took the pilot aboard and then sank the flying boat.

On 22 May Pierozzi and 2º Nocciere Beniamino Piro of *260ª Squadriglia* were on a reconnaissance sortie to Pola when they were intercepted by two Phönix D Is off Rovigno. Although Lang was again leading, this time in A110, the Macchis held their own remarkably well and Pierozzi claimed probable hits on one of the enemy fighters. This was duly confirmed as his sixth victory when it was learned that A115 had force landed offshore with its pilot, Frglt Stefan Wollemann, wounded.

Between combats Pierozzi spent May and June 1918 test flying such types as the Hanriot HD 2 seaplane and the ISVA – a disappointing *'Idrovolanti'* (seaplane) version of the Savoia-Verduzio-Ansaldo SVA 5 fighter/reconnaisance biplane.

When the Austro-Hungarians launched their last push along the Piave on 15 June, Pierozzi led his M.5s in support of the Allied defence and counterthrust. On 2 July large Austrian flying boat K394, escorted by three fighters, was preparing to attack Italian torpedo boats off Caorle when five *260ª Squadriglia* M.5s led by Pierozzi attacked the formation. During the course of the fight Pierozzi brought the bomber down in flames, although its crew, Seefänrich Vinzenz Guglielmi, Flgmt Emil Modler and Fliegermatrose Nieboda, survived to be taken prisoner.

Now Italy's leading naval ace, Pierozzi escorted land bombers on 6 July, after which he strafed an enemy truck and trenches. Following the completion of this mission, M.5 No 18, which he had been flying since April, was retired and he switched to M.5 No 25.

Although struck by anti-aircraft fire on 13 July and 19 August, Pierozzi flew constantly, including night missions in September. Calvello also carried out nocturnal sorties to deliver homing pigeons to spies operating behind enemy lines.

Pola continued to be a tough target for the Italians. On 12 August Friedrich Lang, flying Phönix A117, caught Macchi L.3 No 37 at an

Frglt Stefan Wollemann with Phönix D I A97 at Altura. Outfought and shot down by Orazio Pierozzi on 22 May 1918, he recovered from his wounds in time to bring down US Navy Ens George Ludlow on 21 August for his only victory of the war (*via Aaron Weaver*)

Ens George H Ludlow, seen in portrait and in the cockpit of an M.5, led the first US Navy combat flight from Porto Corsini to Pola on 21 August 1918. Engaging Phönix fighters during the course of the mission, he forced naval ace Friedrich Lang to dive out of the fight but was in turn shot down by Wollemann (*National Archives*)

for home. Wollemann was duly credited with his sole victory of the war. Having turned off his engine as he dived, however, Ludlow extinguished the flames and his Macchi force-landed just five miles from Pola. At that point Hammann landed his own damaged M.5 alongside Ludlow's, and after the latter kicked holes in his hull and wings, took off with Ludlow laying flat on his stomach under the radiator, holding onto the engine mount struts. Ludlow's Macchi sank just as the Austro-Hungarian destroyer *Csikos* arrived to salvage it.

Choppy three-foot swells had so damaged the bow of Hammann's flying boat that it nosed over onto its back upon landing at Porto Corsini, with the pilot trapped by his safety belt until Ludlow dove under and freed him. For rescuing his comrade from the very jaws of the enemy, Charles Hammann became the first American to earn the Medal of Honor for courage above and beyond the call of duty in aerial combat, as well as the Italian *Medaglia d'Argento al Valore Militare*. Tragically, before receiving it Hammann would die in a post-war flying accident in Langley, Virginia, on 21 June 1919. Ludlow received the Navy Cross and the *Medaglia de Bronzo*.

Pierozzi's Macchis again lent their support to the Italian army during the final breakthrough at Vittorio Veneto. While strafing Austro-Hungarian troops near Caorle on 31 October, Calvello's M.5 was struck by return fire and force landed in a swamp. In a reprise of Hammann's feat, Sottotenente di Vascello Ivo Ravazzone landed nearby. After scuttling his flying boat Calvello took over Ravazzone's controls and departed under heavy rifle fire, with Ravazzone hanging onto the engine struts, to fly both men safely to Allied lines.

On 1 November Pierozzi led escorts for a bombing mission to Trieste, then strafed barges in the Marano Canal. Two days later he landed at the once-redoubtable enemy base, as Italian soldiers marched into Trieste.

Recently promoted Ens Charles Hazeltine Hammann poses beside an M.5 of the US Navy squadron at Porto Corsini, resplendent in its late-war livery that included a flying US Navy goat! Hammann flew a less ornate machine on 21 August 1918, when his rescue of Ludlow earned him the Medal of Honor (*National Museum of Naval Aviation*)

On that same day Pierozzi, whose honours included three *Medaglie d'Argento* and one *Bronzo*, took over command of Trieste NAS – the position once held by his Austrian counterpart, Banfield.

In February 1919 Pierozzi, with Prince Ajmone di Savoia – who had flown with *251ᵃ Squadriglia* – visited the Caproni plant in Milan and the SIAI factory at Sesto to see the latter firm's new S.13 flying boat, which would soon win the Schneider Trophy race at Bournemouth with Guido Jannello at the controls. On 17 March Pierozzi and Ajmone left Venice in a Macchi M.9, bound for Trieste, but as they were coming in to land a 'Bora' wind overturned the flying boat. Ajmone emerged with minor bruises, but Orazio Pierozzi suffered head injuries from which he died in the military hospital the next day.

Surviving the war with two *Medaglie d'Argento*, Umberto Calvello flew the mail between Venice and Pola before being assigned to Trieste from 1 December 1918 to 1 June 1919. He then returned to Venice. On 10 August Calvello was test-flying a new SIAI S.9 flying boat when its engine faltered during a steep banking turn and it stalled and crashed in the Venice lagoon. Calvello was killed instantly.

Friedrich Lang formally separated from a Hapsburg navy that no longer existed on 31 March 1919. He is known to have lived into the late 1930s, but there the paper trail vanishes into obscurity.

Unlike many of his fellow naval airmen, Federico Martinengo eschewed post-war service in Italy's independent *Regia Aeronautica* to remain in the *Regia Marina*. In World War 2 he commanded the light cruiser *Muzio Attendolo* at Calabria and other naval battles, rose to the rank of rear admiral and commanded Italy's anti-submarine forces at La Spezia. The day after Italy capitulated to the Allies, on 9 September 1943, Martinengo was aboard *Vas 234* (one of two 70-ton anti-submarine vedettes trying to reach Malta) when they were intercepted by a pair of German minesweepers of the 11th *Räumboot-Flottille*. In the ensuing hour-long running fight, *Vas 234's* helmsman was killed and Martinengo took over, only to fall moments later with a bullet in the brain. Fighting on until its ammunition ran out, *Vas 234* was finally run aground burning near Cala Scirocco, where its crew abandoned the vessel just before it blew up. Thanks to its sacrifice the other vedette, *Vas 235*, escaped.

On 14 September 1943 Martinengo was buried with military honours on Gorgona. To the two *Medaglie d'Argento* and *Croce di Guerra* he had earned in World War 1, his final act of heroism added the *Medaglia d'Oro al Valore Militare*. In the late 1980s, at his wife's request, Martinengo's remains were reinterred at the naval cemetery at La Spezia.

The first of the Adriatic aces was also the longest-lived. Awarded the *Ritterkreuz der Militär Maria-Theresien Orden*, the Hapsburg Empire's highest honour – and with it a baron's title – Gottfried *Freiherr* von Banfield remained in Trieste after the war, acquiring Italian citizenship during the course of a successful life in shipping salvage. In November 1981 he attended the last great World War 1 aces reunion in Paris, the sole Austrian representative hobnobbing with three Hungarians, an Italian and two Canadians who had all served on the Italian front. He remained a tall, elegant gentleman until his death on 23 September 1986, aged 96.

ALLIES IN CAMELS

In addition to the many subjects of the British Empire who achieved distinction in the ranks of the Royal Naval Air Service, the Royal Hellenic Navy produced an ace while operating alongside the RNAS in 1918. Later that year the US Navy's only ace would achieve his success in a former RNAS squadron under RAF auspices.

Aristeides Moraitinis was born in 1891 and joined the Royal Hellenic Navy in 1910. When the First Balkan War broke out on 5 October 1912, he was executive officer of Torpedo Boat No 15. He got his first taste of aviation during the Second Balkan War, when on 6 February 1913, he flew as observer in a Maurice Farman MF 7 seaplane piloted by Greek army officer 1Lt Michael Moutousis on a reconnaissance flight over the Dardenelles. He dropped four grenades on the Turks during the mission, which ended when engine trouble forced the Farman down. The seaplane had to be towed back to Mudros by the destroyer *Velos*.

Ens Moraitinis' taste for flying was whetted, and when the navy invited officers to take flight training, he was among the first three to volunteer. On 22 September 1914 he received British pilot's certificate No 1087 at Eleussis naval station after soloing in a Sopwith hydroplane. Not long after, Lt Moraitinis was put in charge of a squadron of four Henry Farman HF 22s, conducting pilot training himself.

At that time Greece was officially neutral at the insistence of King Constantine I, whose wife Sofia was Kaiser Wilhelm II's sister. The presence of foreign soldiers battling it out on their home soil in Salonika, however, stirred widespread Greek resentment toward the Central Powers, and after resigning twice (on 5 March and 5 October 1915) Prime Minister Eleftheios Venizelos formed an alternative government on Crete and offered up some 20,000 troops in three divisions to fight alongside the Allies. Moraitinis threw his lot in with the pro-Allied camp, and by late 1916 he was instructing airmen for the Naval Flying Corps (NFC), using what he called 'training by personal experience', which involved combat sorties.

On 9 March 1917 Moraitinis carried out a raid against the Bulgarians on the Salonika front. Even more notable was a sortie on the 31st, when he and 2Lt Pantelis Psyhas departed Thasos in a Henry Farman HF 27 for a night raid on the Bulgarian-German aerodrome at Zerevic. Striking

Besides being credited with nine victories, Aristeides Moraitinis was a pioneer naval flier who also carried out training, reconnaissance and bombing assignments with equal zeal and fearlessness – in essence, the heart and soul of Hellenic naval aviation (*Hellenic Air Force via Thomas Zacharis*)

Although seven Sopwith Hydro Biplane Type Ss were ordered for the Royal Hellenic Naval Flying Corps by Lt(jg) Moraitinis and British Cdr Collyns Price Pizey, only one was delivered in May 1914, with a 100 hp Anzani radial engine that gave it a speed of 55 mph. Operating from Eleusis Naval Station, Moraitinis and several other early Greek aviators-in-training cut their teeth on the 'Greek Seaplane' before it crashed during a training flight that July (*Museum of the History of Aviation via Thomas Zacharis*)

from an altitude of 500 ft, they set the hangars on fire, then attacked the railway station at Drama, destroying three trains with one well-placed 100-lb bomb. This earned Moraitinis a citation from the British as a 'fearless aviator'.

In May Moraitinis' NFC contingent was organised as an independent component of 2 Naval Wing under the title of 'Z' (Greek) Squadron, operating its HF 27s with its own fighter escort of Bristol Scout Cs over the Macedonian front. As strikes and counterstrikes between the opposing air arms escalated, the British replaced the obsolescent Farmans with 14 Sopwith 1½ Strutters, along with two Sopwith Camels.

A poor-quality but highly evocative photograph of Lt Moraitinis in a Henry Farman HF 27 of 'Z' (Greek) Squadron of 2 Naval Wing RNAS returning to base at Lesbos at dusk following a bombing raid on Smyrna in the spring of 1917 (*Hellenic Air Force*)

Under pressure, particularly from the French, to drop his nominally neutralist, tacitly pro-German stand, King Constantine I finally abdicated the throne on 11 June, to be replaced by his second son, Alexander. When Greece formally declared war on the Central Powers on 29 June 1917, the NFC's operations expanded to attacking its long-standing enemies, the Turks, in the Dardanelles. In the wake of one such bombing raid, the British awarded Lt Moraitinis the DSO.

After some time training pilots in Thasos, Lt Cdr Moraitinis was reassigned to Mudros in early January 1918. He arrived just in time to participate in the first major air battle of the year – the Allied attempt to destroy the battlecruiser *Yavuz Sultan Selim*. Bearing this name for only a short time, the vessel was actually the ex-German *Goeben*, which with the light cruiser *Breslau* had slipped past the Royal Navy to be presented to the Turks – an act that influenced the Ottoman Empire's fateful decision to ally itself with the Central Powers in 1914. Since then, *Yavuz* and *Midilli* (as *Breslau* was renamed), still crewed primarily by German personnel, had adversely affected the balance of power in

This rare photograph, taken in 1915, shows Lt Aristeides Moraitinis, shorn of the beard he wore in most portraits, at left, with fellow Greek pilot Dimitrios Chadjiskos. Later rejoining the fleet, Chadjiskos was serving as commander of the destroyer *Niki* when he was killed by Turkish fire while evacuating troops from Eritrea on 17 September 1922 (*Hellenic Maritime Museum*)

the Black Sea and the Eastern Mediterranean, intermittently striking at Russian and British bases and having several engagements with the Russian Black Sea Fleet.

On the morning of 20 January, *Yavuz* and *Midilli* attacked the British naval base at Imbros Island, setting fire to airfield installations and sinking the monitors *Raglan* and *M28*. Coming under attack by Imbros-based aeroplanes, the warships ran into a minefield and five mines exploded against *Midilli,* sinking her. *Yavuz* struck three mines, but steamed back

towards the Dardanelles, pursued both by aircraft and the destroyers HMS *Lizard* and *Tigress*. Among the first Allied airmen over *Yavuz* was Moraitinis, who, flying a Camel, came under anti-aircraft fire – he hoped to distract enemy attention from a British submarine in the near vicinity. While he was refuelling on Imbros, *Yavuz* ran aground on a sandbank at Nagara Point.

When Moraitinis returned to the Dardanelles, the beached warship was under attack from two Mudros-based Blackburn-built Sopwith Baby floatplanes of 6 Naval Wing, each carrying a 65-lb bomb. As they neared *Yavuz* the British aircraft were attacked by German fighters of *Fl Abt* 6. One of the Babys was shot down in flames by Ltn Emil Meinecke, killing Flt Sub-Lt William Johnston.

Pressing on, Flt Sub-Lt Robert W Peel flew over *Yavuz*, only to discover his bomb would not release. He then turned and made another pass despite being pursued by enemy aeroplanes, managing to drop his bomb close alongside *Yavuz*. Peel's engine then lost power and he force landed just aft of the battlecruiser. The engine picked up again, however, and he was able to alternately fly and taxi his way back to Imbros. On 14 September Peel was gazetted for the DSC for his courageous persistence.

Meanwhile, Moraitinis was hotly engaged with ten Turkish aircraft. In a conversation with fellow pilot Konstantinos Panagiotou, he described what occurred;

'I spotted a German aeroplane, but when I attempted to shoot at him my machine gun jammed. I turned off my engine and started to drop, and when I thought that he had lost me I levelled my aeroplane and started to repair the machine gun. As soon as I unjammed it, I started to climb, and then there was another German ahead. I attacked him, and in a short while I saw him going down. Although I was certain by the way he was falling that he had no hope, I wanted to make sure, but in the meantime I saw another one approaching. I attacked him also, but as I attempted to check that I had indeed shot him down, I heard my engine spluttering and, shortly after, it stalled. Fortunately, the propeller still continued to turn.

'I started to come down in a glide somewhere between the Straits and Marvia, and I was beginning to lose hope when I heard the sound of a machine gun behind me. I turned and saw a German shooting at me. I was at an altitude of only 800 metres. Once more, and full of despair, I tried to switch my engine on again and curiously enough this time it worked. You can understand what happened then! I was immediately on his tail, and I did not lose him until I saw him going down and disappearing.'

After managing to limp back to Imbros with 20 holes in his aeroplane, including one through the fuel tank and struts, Moraitinis flew a third two-hour sortie in another Camel. Disregarding his insistance that he should not 'say a word about anything we cannot prove', 'Kosta' Panagiotou passed his combat account on to the

Powered by a Clerget 9B engine, Sopwith Camel B6360 was delivered to 2 Naval Wing RNAS at Mudros on 31 October 1917, and it was still there on 12 January 1918, suggesting that it may have been seconded to 'Z' (Greek) Squadron for a time, including during the *'Goeben* Affair'. It was at the Mudros repair base in June and officially assigned to Greek squadron H2 between October 1918 and January 1919 (*Hellenic Maritime Museum*)

Groundcrewmen work on Sopwith Camel B3769 of D Sqn, 2 Naval Wing RNAS at Stavros in November 1917. B3769 was successively operated by 2 Naval Wing and No 222 Sqn RAF, before being transferred to Royal Hellenic naval squadron H2 in December 1918 (*Fleet Air Arm Museum JMB/GSL03769*)

British and Greek authorities. Turkish records later revealed that they had lost two 'reconnaissance aeroplanes' that day.

With *Yavuz* immobilised, the British had a golden opportunity to destroy the most powerful warship in the Aegean – and for the next five days they and the Greeks sent every aeroplane they could muster against it. Moraitinis alternated between piloting fighters and bombers during the course of this maximum effort.

Yavuz had no anti-aircraft guns aboard, so the Turks and Germans had to deploy them nearby on land. Their nearest aerodrome, at Chanak-Kale (Canakkale in Turkish), was home to a German seaplane unit, or *Wasser Flieger Abteilung*, and reconnaissance detachments from *Fl Abt* 1 and *Fl Abt* 6. The latter included two Fokker E IIIs, two Halberstadt D Vs and two Albatros D IIIs within their ranks. Like the Allies, the Germans and Turks sent up everything they had in defence of the vessel, and they managed to take a toll of the attackers. On the 20 January, for example, Ltn Emil Meinecke of *Fl Abt* 6 was credited with Johnston's Baby off Nagara Point, while Ltn Schubert of the *Wasser Flieger Abteilung* claimed two victories (possibly both Johnston and Peel).

Bad weather aided the defenders' cause on the 21st, but the Allied air attacks resumed in earnest on the 22nd. On this date Meinecke had an inconclusive fight with a Camel, which may have been flown by Moraitinis. On the 23rd Meinecke shot down a 1½ Strutter in flames, the body of the aeroplane's pilot, Greek Flt Sub-Lt Spyros Hambas, being recovered off Chanak-Kale.

Finally, on the night of 26 January, the Turkish pre-dreadnought *Torgut Reis* managed to help free *Yavuz* from the shore and then tow it to Constantinople, where the vessel would still be under repair when the war ended. The Allies had flown a total of 276 sorties and dropped 15 tons of explosives on the stranded warship, losing about 20 aircraft and only achieving two small bomb hits on the target for all their trouble.

In retrospect, the air battle over Nagara represented a lost opportunity for aeroplanes to destroy a capital ship before American Brig Gen William Mitchell's peacetime demonstration of air power on 21 July 1921. Equally significant, however, was the role aircraft had played in the warship's survival.

The Greeks, too, had proven their mettle, and by May 1918 the British were giving them more independence in their conduct of operations, while helping the NFC expand into four squadrons in the Aegean – H1 at Thasos, H2 at Mudros, H3 at Savroupolis and H4 at Mitilinoi. Moraitinis commanded H2, whose mixed bag of aircraft included Bristol Scout Ds, Pups and Camels.

In July the Turks launched a wave of air attacks on the islands of Mytilene, Chios and Samos. In response, on 13 July Moraitinis led a small detachment of H2 aircraft to Kalloni, on Lesbos. Besides intercepting the raiders, Moraitinis and his six pilots struck at Turkish

This line up of aircraft assigned to Royal Hellenic naval squadron H2 at Mudros in late 1918 includes (from right) five Camels, two Pups, three DH 4s and a DH 9 (*Hellenic Maritime Museum*)

Not merely assigned to H2, DH 9 E8991 was presented personally to its CO in full Greek markings, including a flag on the fuselage side and a small plaque reading *To the Commander A Moraitinis DSO* (*Museum of the History of Aviation Thomas Zacharis*)

airfields and installations at Magnesia, Chanak-Kale and Smyrna. The Greek aeroplanes often returned riddled by anti-aircraft fire, and after flying a raid on 22 July in spite of a faulty engine, which compelled him to fly low over Kazimir airfield, Moraitinis was exhorted by both the Naval Ministry and the high commissioner of Lesbos to curb his reckless behaviour.

At the end of July operations from Kalloni concluded, and Moraitinis reunited his detachment with the rest of H2 at Mudros, from which it would operate for the rest of the war. By its conclusion, Moraitinis had logged a total of 185 combat missions, comprising 80 bombing, 27 reconnaissance, 25 maritime patrol and 18 fighter sweeps. He had engaged in 20 aerial combats during these missions, and was credited with nine victories. Moraitinis' exploits in two wars earned him numerous Greek honours, as well as the British DSO and his very own DH 9, E8991, bearing the presentation inscription *To the Commander A Moraitinis DSO*.

Although he had survived the war, Moraitinis' illustrious career in Greek naval aviation came to a tragically premature end. At noon on 22 December 1918 he took off from Thessaloniki, bound for Athens, in a Breguet 14 that was the personal transport of Commandant Victor Denain, the French CO of the Inter-Allied Air Force. Besides putting his aeroplane at his disposal, Denain had, in view of Mortainis' unfamiliarity with the type, also assigned a French mechanic to accompany him. Moraitinis, however, turned down the offer and took off solo. He never reached his destination, and it is believed that he crashed in the sea somewhere between Halkidiki and Magnesia.

As with Greece's Moraitinis, the war's only US Navy ace flew with the British. Like the USAS, the US Navy had numerous fighter designs in the works but had to rely on foreign-built machines for its squadrons in World War I There was a fighter squadron at Dunkirk, in France, equipped with Hanriot HD 2 seaplanes, and another based in Porto Corsini, in Italy, operating Macchi M.5 and M.7 flying boats. In addition, the US Navy assigned pilots to temporary duty with French naval *escadrilles* at Dunkirk, and with RAF fighter and bomber squadrons along the Flanders coast. It was in one of the latter units that David Ingalls got the chance to show his mettle in combat.

Born in Cleveland, Ohio, on 28 January 1899, David Sinton Ingalls Jr entered aviation as part of the First Yale Unit. This was a training contingent made up primarily of the social elite – Ingalls' father, David S Ingalls, was an executive of the New York Central Railroad, and his mother, Jane Taft Ingalls, was the niece of former President William Howard Taft.

Entering Yale University in 1916, Ingalls enlisted in the US Naval Reserve on 26 March 1917 and then enrolled for its Flying Corps. Training in civilian seaplanes at West Palm Beach, Florida, followed by naval instruction at Huntington, Long Island, Ingalls duly qualified as a pilot on 14 August and obtained his ensign's commission on 4 September. After a short stint participating in anti-submarine detection testing at New London, Connecticut, he and six fellow Yale Unit members departed for England aboard the transport vessel *Philadelphia* on 23 September.

A newly commissioned Ens David Sinton Ingalls proudly displays his new ensign's shoulder boards while undergoing flight training. He went on to pilot flying boats, bombers and Hanriot HD 2 seaplane fighters, as well as land-based fighters, during the course of his wartime career (*Courtesy Peter B Mersky Collection*)

The first three fighter-trained members of the 'First Yale Unit' at the time of their assignment to 13 Naval Squadron RNAS in late March 1918. They are, from left to right, Ens Edward 'Shorty' Smith, David 'Crock' Ingalls and Kenneth MacLeish (*Fleet Air Arm Museum JMB/GSL07539*)

From London, the seven Yale men were despatched to Paris, where four were ordered to the US naval air station at Moutchic to crew flying boats. 'Crock' Ingalls, as his comrades nicknamed him, was among the three who lost the coin toss and spent the next few months, as he described it, 'playing bridge' and 'eating, I think, and drinking in all the funny little restaurants in Paris'. Ingalls' ennui ended on 13 December when he and his two comrades were picked to be flight leaders in a future naval fighter squadron. They were duly sent to Gosport Flying School in England to train on Avro 504s and Sopwith Pups and Camels, followed by further training in Ayr, Scotland. There, Ingalls made the acquaintance of a number of USAS trainees, including future fighter ace and author Elliott White Springs and bomber pilot and artist Clayton Knight.

On 21 March 1918 Ingalls finally commenced a combat assignment at US Naval Air Station (USNAS) St Pol-sur-Mer, under the command of Lt Godfrey Chevalier. Attached to the US Navy's Northern Bombing Group, Ingalls flew Hanriot HD 2s along the Flanders coast until, in view of the German offensive that had just plunged into British lines, Chevalier offered some of his pilots to the RNAS. In consequence Ens Ingalls, Kenneth MacLeish and Edward R Smith, as well as former *Escadrille Lafayette* member-turned US Navy Lt Willis B Haviland, were assigned to 13 Naval Squadron under the command of Sqn Cdr Ronald Graham. Based at Berques, nine kilometres south of Dunkirk, the unit

This photograph of Camels of No 213 Sqn lends some credibility to Ingalls' claim that his aeroplane, at least, bore no distinctive markings. C73, in which he scored his first victory on 11 August 1918, may have been similar to the aeroplane in the background (*Fleet Air Arm Museum JMB/GSL06388*)

became No 213 Sqn RAF, on 1 April – the day before Ingalls made his first Camel flight with the unit.

'The Sopwith Camel was the slowest of the better fighters', Ingalls said in an interview some years after the war. 'It couldn't run away from a fight, so that once you were actually involved you stayed until something happened one way or the other. At least you had a machine that would turn inside the other aeroplane and give you a chance that I thought was better than simply speed, which would enable you to dive safely away'.

Ingalls also stated that 'the machine guns were one of our greatest difficulties due to a faulty timing mechanism or something similar. They would shoot seven or eight times at most before misfiring. The pilot would then have to hit the handle of the loading apparatus and reload, and then his gun could shoot again for seven or eight times'.

Ingalls spent April performing low fleet patrols and bomber escort missions until the 20th, when he was discharged to USNAS Dunkirk. More school work and languishing followed until 9 July, when he arrived at No 218 Sqn RAF for two weeks of bombing missions in DH 9s. Later that month he was recalled to the Northern Bombing Group, where he was promoted to lieutenant junior grade.

After about a week of putting in requests, Ingalls obtained reassignment to No 213 Sqn on 9 August. In his letters home he described life there as 'exceedingly pleasant', and that 'quarters and food were of the best'. He noted that the pilots spent much of their spare time shooting, and impressed on him their credo that marksmanship was paramount over good eyesight and flying ability for a successful fighter pilot. 'This was forcibly brought home to me when three of us dove at a two-seater spotting across the lines', he wrote. 'We were all together in the dive, and before I thought we were in range, the Hun suddenly burst into flames. The flight commander had hit him from what we afterwards agreed must have been at least 400 or 500 yards'.

Usually flying two missions per day, Ingalls much preferred offensive patrols to the low sweeps the unit made to guard the coastal destroyer patrols from attacks from Zeebrugge and Ostende. 'As there were seldom any enemy seaplanes to be seen, and one always looked forward to a cold bath if the motor failed, this was rather a stupid job', Ingalls wrote.

At 0855 hrs on 11 August he took off for a high offensive patrol (HOP). An hour later, he and 19-year-old Dulwich College-educated Lt Colin Peter Brown spotted an Albatros two-seater at 10,000 ft. The German dove away toward Ostende, pursued by Brown and Ingalls, who fired 150 rounds in short bursts until they disengaged seven miles northeast of Dixmude. 'Just after the Camels broke off combat', the narrative stated, 'the enemy aeroplane went into a low spin which gradually became faster and faster, and was last seen spinning about 1000 ft from the ground, obviously out of control'. The two-seater's demise was jointly credited as Brown's sixth victory – of an eventual 14 – and Ingalls' first.

On 13 August No 213 Sqn's Camels, including Ingalls in N6376, joined No 210 Sqn and the USAS's 17th Aero Squadron, as well as the DH 9s of Nos 211 and 218 Sqns, in the attack on Varssenaere aerodrome, with Camels of No 204 Sqn flying high cover. During his second HOP on 21 August Ingalls teamed up with the just-promoted Capt Brown and Lt Harry C Smith to attack an LVG south of Zevecote. After diving after the enemy aeroplane from 7000 ft down to 3000 ft, during which time Ingalls fired 100 rounds at it from 150 yards, the trio disengaged due to anti-aircraft fire, but the LVG was seen diving steeply, issuing black smoke, until it hit the ground.

In a third sortie that evening, nine of No 213 Sqn's Camels, including Ingalls, intercepted two Brandenburg W 29 seaplanes escorted by nine Fokker D VIIs of the *Seefrontstaffel*. Gray shot one of the Fokkers down into the sea, killing Flgmt Friedrich Gröschke, but 2Lt J Wooding was brought down (probably by Flgmt Hubrich) off Zeebrugge and taken prisoner. Lt W A Rankin's Camel was also disabled, although he made it to Allied lines before safely force landing. His immobilization was credited to either Flgmt Kairies or Ltn Becht.

Ingalls' next chance to score occurred on 15 September after a 20-aeroplane bombing raid on Uytkerke aerodrome. During the return flight he and Harry Smith attacked a Rumpler east of Ostende pier, and they reported that after firing 400 rounds at the aeroplane it went down out of control and on fire.

'A last look showed him crashing into the water by the beach', Ingalls wrote home, 'and Smith joined me above the clouds. He had seen the Hun burst into flames and crash through a break, and we went home rejoicing. A minute later our commanding officer, who, on seeing the Hun and the scrap, had turned back, joined us and waved'.

On the 18th Ingalls' letter to his father detailed the activities of the past few days;

'This morning I led my flight – note the nonchalant way I say "my flight" – over the coast and we got a kite balloon in flames. Pretty nice, eh? It was very pretty, for just as it caught fire the two observers jumped with beautiful white parachutes. Luckily the burning balloon fell on three hangars below, and there was some fire. We contour-chased home just over the ground, and I managed to set fire to some barracks a little way behind the lines.'

The balloon, hit at 4000 ft as its crew tried to winch it down, fell near La Barrière. Credit was shared between Ingalls, Smith and Lt George S Hodson.

On 20 September, as 15 Camels escorted DH 9s of No 218 Sqn over Varssenaere, four Fokker D VIIs approached the formation at 15,500 ft. Ingalls, flying Camel D8177, led his flight head-on at the enemy, almost collided with the German leader and fought him until the fighter dived away. Rejoining the bombers, he noticed one straggling with an ailing motor that was attracting the attention of two Fokkers.

'I approached at right angles, and deciding that the first-named Hun was the most dangerous, fired at him from the right', Ingalls wrote. 'He immediately went down with smoke coming out of his machine, so I turned and went after the other Hun. He could not have seen me, for I got within about 30 yards and then had a perfect shot at thim. I don't know how I could have missed, for I almost ran into him. He turned over onto his back and went into a spin'.

Three more attacking Fokkers occupied Ingalls' attention after that, but he scattered them and then turned to rejoin his formation 'while these three beggars kept shooting from an impossible distance until I crossed the coast'. The first Fokker he sent down smoking over Vlisseghem was confirmed as his ace-making fifth victory, but No 213 Sqn witnesses claimed to have seen the other pull out of its spin.

On 24 September Ingalls, in Camel D9649, and four others took on 12 Fokkers between Couckelaere and Thorout at 1450 hrs. Capt Brown claimed two as crashed, while Hodson got one out of control and another crashed. Ingalls drove one off Smith's tail. Up again at 1645 hrs on a test flight with Hodson, Ingalls spotted an enemy aeroplane over Nieuwpoort. Giving chase, the Camels caught up with the intruder over St Pierre Capelle. 'The Hun was an old Rumpler, the slowest I ever saw', Ingalls wrote, 'and he just kept on, so I dove under him and came up below. But he was so slow that I overshot, and could not train my guns on him. So I dove again and tried once more. He would turn one way to give his observer a shot and I could try to keep under him, making a bigger circle, so his observer would not shoot'.

After several such frustrating passes while the Rumpler flew over its own lines, Ingalls said, 'I gave up the careful, cautious tactics, got straight behind him and kept firing for probably 100 rounds'. That last attack was rewarded with 'a big puff of smoke' from the Rumpler's engine, and Ingalls raced for home at low altitude. His aeroplane had also been struck by machine gun fire, and he limped back to Berques on six cylinders with his main fuel tank holed and some flying wires severed. Hodson also returned. 'He said that he had been back of and above me, and had fired from there and seen the Hun burst into flames and crash', Ingalls wrote. 'So we felt fine, and I got a new machine the next day'.

Assigned Camel F3239, Ingalls scored no further successes before 3 October, when he was discharged to RNAS Dunkirk. He spent the rest of the war as a ferry pilot and as an instructor at Eastleigh. During his time with No 213 Sqn Ingalls had flown 63 combat missions, been credited with six victories and was awarded the RAF's DFC, with an added remark from his CO, Maj Graham;

'His keenness, courage and utter disregard of danger are an example to all. He is one of the finest men this squadron ever had'.

That was high praise, coming as it did from a man who had been with No 213 Sqn from its formative days as the Seaplane Defence Flight, and who would score his fifth victory – an LVG in flames – on 19 October. In addition to his British honours, Ingalls received the US Navy's DSM.

After pursuing a post-war law career, David Ingalls served from 1926 to 1928 as a representative in the Ohio Legislature and co-sponsored the Ohio Aviation Code (*Jon Guttman*)

On 27 September, while recovering from a bout of flu, Lt Kenneth MacLeish had written home;

'Dave Ingalls got another Hun! That makes three Huns and two balloons. Isn't he the luckiest stiff who ever lived. How does he rate all that flying when his old sidekick has to sit here and do nothing except get sick? I'm jealous, to be perfectly frank. I'm darned jealous'.

With Ingalls' transfer to Eastleigh, MacLeish was assigned to take his place in No 213 Sqn. His tour with the unit, however, was to prove tragically short-lived. On 14 October the unit became embroiled in at least two sprawling dogfights with MFJ IV, which claimed five Camels, four Dolphins and two balloons for the loss of Ltn z S Stinsky. Among the actual British losses were six of No 213 Sqn's Camels, with all of their pilots killed, including Lt MacLeish.

After the war Ingalls completed his education at Yale in 1920, studied law at Harvard and became a lawyer thereafter. From 1926 to 1928 he was a representative in the Ohio Legislature and co-sponsored the Ohio Aviation Code. President Herbert Hoover subsequently appointed him Assistant Secretary of the Navy for Aeronautics.

As Assistant Secretary of the Navy for Aeronautics under President Herbert Hoover's administration, Ingalls had a Curtiss A-4 – a civilian version of the F8C-8 Helldiver with an enclosed canopy – as his personal aeroplane. He is shown here in 1929 with humorist Will Rogers at left (*Courtesy Peter B Mersky Collection*)

Returning to the US Navy in World War 2, Cdr Ingalls helped form the Naval Air Transport System and, in 1943, he became chief of staff for the Forward Area Air Center at Guadalcanal. He retired from the Navy with the rank of rear admiral on 8 November 1945, and from the Naval Reserve on 1 February 1959. Ingalls subsequently worked as vice president of Pan American Airways, and as president and publisher of the Cincinnati *Times-Star* newspaper. Inducted into the Naval Aviation Hall of Fame in 1983, David Ingalls died in Chagrin Falls, Ohio, on 26 April 1985.

APPENDICES

German Naval Aces

Pilot	Unit/s	Score
Paul Achilles	SFS 2, MFJ V	11
Eduard Blaas	MFJ II, III	5
Erich Bönisch (Obs)	SFL	15
Albin Bühl	SFS 1, MFJ IV	6
Friedrich Christiansen	SFL 1	13
Karl Engelfried	SFS 2, MFJ IV	5
Hans Goerth	MFJ I, III	7
Bertram Heinrich	MFJ I	12
Gerhard Hubrich	SFS 1, MFJ IV	12
Christian Kairies	SFS 1, MFJ IV	6
Karl Kutsche	SFS 2, MFJ V	5
Karl Maier	SFI 1, MFJ	18
Konrad Mettlich	MFJ I, *Jasta* 8	6
Theodor Osterkamp	MFJ I, II	32
Reinhold Poss	SFS 1, MFJ IV	11
Gotthard Sachsenberg	MFJ I, Marine JGr	31
Karl Scharon	MFJ II	8
Kurt Schönfelder	*Jasta* 7	13
Wilhelm Thöne	MFJ I	5
Alexander Zenses	MFJ II	18

COLOUR PLATES

Artist Harry Dempsey has created the colour profiles for this volume, working closely with the author to portray the aircraft as accurately as circumstances permit. Some of the illustrations are, admittedly, reconstructions based on fragmentary photographic evidence or descriptions provided by the pilots while they were alive, combined with known unit marking policy.

1

Friedrichshafen FF 33H Nr 599 of Flgobmt Karl Meyer and Ltn z S Erich Bönisch, *Seeflugstation* 1, Zeebrugge, Belgium, July 1916

Flgobmt Karl Meyer and Ltn z S Erich Bönisch were flying in this seaplane when they brought down a French FBA flying boat on 17 July 1916. They also used it to drive a Caudron G 4 down behind Allied lines near Ostende on 2 August. Three days later, in Hansa-Brandenburg LW Nr 571, they shot down another FBA off Middlekerke. The latter was Meyer's third victory and Bönisch's fifth.

2

Rumpler 6B 1 Nr 788 of Flgmstr Karl Meyer, *Seeflugstation* 1, Zeebrugge, Belgium, February 1917

Based on Rumpler's successful C I reconnaissance aeroplane, the 6B 1 was a seaplane fighter with added wing stagger to accommodate the redistribution of weight due to its single-seat configuration. Accepted for service on 10 August 1916, the aeroplane was powered by a 160 hp Mercedes D III engine and armed with a synchronised LMG 08/15 machine gun. Limited range for escort duties and the initial weakness of the 6B 1's rudder control attachment limited production to just 35 examples, although another 50 6B 2s with twin machine guns were also produced. On 1 February 1917 Flgmstr Karl Meyer was flying the third prototype, Marine Nr 788, when he brought down Sopwith Pup N6161 at Breedene, near Blankenberge, for his sixth victory. Flt Sub-Lt G L Elliott of 'Naval 3' was taken prisoner.

3

Hansa-Brandenburg W 12 Nr 1183 of Oblt z S Friedrich Christiansen, *Seeflugstation* 1, Zeebrugge, Belgium, October 1917

On 1 October 1917 Christiansen, in W 12 Nr 1183, with Ltn z S Hillger as his observer, drove a Felixstowe-based Porte FB 2 Baby flying boat down off Texel. This was confirmed as Christiansen's second victory, despite the fact that its crew, Flt Cdr N S Douglas and Flt Lt B D Hobbs, taxied the flying boat back to England. On 11 December Christiansen, with Flgmt Bernhard Wladicka as his observer, and the patrol he led shared in the destruction of Astra-Torres airship C27, killing Flt Lts John F Dixon DFC and Herbert Fail, AM2 John C Collett and AM1s James E Martin and Ernest R White. That same day Christiansen received the *Orden Pour le Mérite*. He was still flying W 12 Nr 1183 when he destroyed a Curtiss H-12B for his fourth victory on 15 February 1918, and on

21 April when he attacked the 127-ton Dutch motor vessel *Meeuw*, setting the vessel alight and sinking it 12 miles off Nord Hinder lightship despite Dutch neutrality. This was destined not to be the last notorious incident with the Netherlands in which Christiansen would be involved.

4

Hansa-Brandenburg W 29 Nr 2512 of Oblt z S Friedrich Christiansen, *Seeflugstation* 1, Zeebrugge, Belgium, July 1918

Ernst Heinkel designed the monoplane W 29 largely at Friedrich Christiansen's suggestion for a W 12 successor, and the future ace was so pleased when he flew the prototype that he wanted to take it into combat immediately. He was certainly flying a W 29 when he scored his fifth through thirteenth confirmed victories, which included British submarine *C25* on 6 July 1918 – even though it was not, in fact, sunk. As with his earlier Friedrichshafen and Hansa-Brandenburg W 12 seaplanes, Christiansen's W 29 bore his initial in a diamond within a diagonal band.

5

Albatros D V (serial unknown) of Flgmt Bertram Heinrich, MFJ I, Aertrycke, Belgium, Autumn 1917

Among the most successful German naval fighter pilots in 1917, Bertram Heinrich was credited with a Sopwith Camel on 11 September 1917 and two SPADs on 21 October, bringing his tally to nine. He would score only thrice more in 1918 before being shot down and killed, probably by Lt William S Jenkins of No 210 Sqn, on 31 August.

6

Pfalz D IIIa Nr 5940/17 of Flgmt Carl Kuring, MFJ II, Jabbeke, Belgium, March 1918

Immediately upon joining MFJ I on 6 November 1917, Flgmt Kuring was transferred to MFJ II, and was later photographed in Pfalz D IIIa Nr 5940/18, which had a yellow band starting midway under the cockpit and a white tail. On 15 May 1918 he was credited with a 'Sopwith Pup' northwest of Oostkerke, which may have been Adj Jules Goossens of the *7éme Escadrille Belge* – he returned unhurt from a combat over Dixmude. That was followed by a DH 9 of No 98 Sqn on 1 June. Subsequently flying Fokker D VIIs, Kuring survived the war, just missing ace status with a total of four victories to his name.

7

Albatros D Va (serial unknown) of Ltn d R z S Theodor Osterkamp, MFJ II, Aertrycke, Belgium, April 1918

Theo Osterkamp described his aircraft as being marked like a 'bumblebee', but there has been little in the way of photographic evidence from which to interpret what he meant! One Albatros that he possibly flew, which crashed sometime in the spring of 1918, had a black-yellow-black fuselage band and what appears to have been a black semi-ellipse on the nose. Otherwise, it seems to have featured standard purple and green stippled camouflage on its wings. As CO of MFJ II, Osterkamp may have extended his black and yellow 'bumblebee' bands over the entire fuselage of his Fokker D VII, as Gotthard Sachsenberg had done with his yellow-black diamond pattern.

8

Albatros D Va Nr 7435/18 of Ltn z S Reinhold Poss, *Seefrontstaffel*, Vlisseghem, Belgium, May 1918

Reinhold Poss opened his account with two Sopwith Babies on 4 May 1918, and three days later he was given command of the *Seefrontstaffel's* second flight. On the 21st he was credited with a Bristol F 2B, followed by a DH 4 of No 217 Sqn on 28 June and a DH 9 of No 218 Sqn on 16 July, but he was himself forced to land near Mariakerke by a Camel on 30 July. On 1 September Poss was given command of the newly formed MFJ IV, with which unit he raised his score to 11, including three Camels of No 213 Sqn on 14 October, before being shot down and taken prisoner the next day. Poss was killed on 26 August 1933 when his aeroplane collided with a church steeple.

9

Albatros D Va (serial unknown) of Flgmt Albin Bühl, *Seefrontstaffel*, Vlisseghem, Belgium, May 1918

On 8 May 1918, '*König*' Bühl was credited with driving a DH 4 into the sea off Nieuwpoort for his third victory. Bühl's nickname was reflected in the 'crown' he applied around the fuselage of his aeroplanes as a personal marking. Later flying Fokker D VIIs with MFJ IV, he survived the war with six victories to his name.

10

Albatros D Va Nr 7167/18 of Flgmt Hans Goerth, MFJ III, Jabbeke, Belgium, June 1918

Hans Goerth had served with *Kustenstaffel* III prior to his transfer to MFJ I on 26 February 1918, but he did not score his first confirmed victory until about a week after joining newly formed MFJ III, when he downed a DH 4 of No 98 Sqn near Mariakerke on 30 June 1918. Goerth noted that he was flying Albatros D Va Nr 7167/18, which bore the legend *Lu* on a white fuselage band. He also used the aeroplane when he scored his second victory (a DH 9 of No 206 Sqn) on 7 July.

11

Fokker E V Nr 160/18(?) of Ltn z S Gotthard Sachsenberg, MFJ I, Jabbeke, Belgium, August 1918

The delivery of new Fokker E V 'Parasol' monoplanes to the *Marine Jagdgruppe* provoked a mixed reaction from pilots, but the commander, Ltn z S Gotthard Sachsenberg, was delighted with the aeroplane and quickly had it decorated with the same yellow and black diamond livery as his D VII. He may have flown it operationally, but not for long before fatal incidents attributed to wing failures at *Jastas* 19 and 6 led to a general order grounding the E Vs from 20 August.

12

Fokker D VII Nr 5492/18 of Flgmstr Hans Goerth, MFJ III, Jabbeke, Belgium, October 1918

Based on a newly discovered photograph showing MFJ III Fokkers, including Goerth's black heart-decorated Albatros-built D VII, and information regarding the fighter's likely serial,

this profile features the aeroplane that was used by Goerth to down a DH 4 of No 108 Sqn and an escorting Camel of No 210 Sqn on 1 October 1918. These were his sixth and seventh (and final) victories of the war.

13

Fokker D VII (serial unknown) of Flgmt Gerhard Hubrich, MFJ IV, Jabbeke, Belgium, October 1918

Another Albatros-built machine appearing in the same photograph as Goerth's Fokker D VII of MFJ III, Hubrich's MFJ IV aeroplane is less easy to make out, but apparently it bears the *'Kuken'* (chick) personal marking based on his nickname. This also appeared on his Albatros D Va D 5815/17, which was assigned to the *Seefrosta* prior to SFS I's expansion into MFJ IV in September 1918. Hubrich survived the war with a total of eight victories to his name.

14

Fokker D VII (serial unknown) of Obflgmstr Kurt Schönfelder, *Jasta* 7, Ste Marguerite, Belgium, June 1918

A naval member of army *Jasta* 7 since December 1916, *'Wassermann'* Schönfelder had become its second-ranking ace with 13 victories by the time he was killed on 26 June 1918. The fuselages of Schönfelder's Albatros D V and later Fokker D VII bore the all-black scheme of *Jasta* 7, with his personal marking of a 'gold star'.

15

Shchetinin M-9 NR-50 of Lt Aleksandr N P de Seversky, 2nd Naval Bomber-Reconnaissance Detachment, Zerel, Russia, August 1916

Designed by Dmitry P Grigorovich, the slow but robust M-9 had some remarkable successes in aerial combat, none more so than those scored by one-legged Lt Aleksandr de Seversky. On 4 July 1916 he was credited with downing an Albatros C Ia over the Gulf of Riga and on 13 August he scored the first triple victory haul by a Russian pilot with three more C Ias – two of them shared – over Lake Angern.

16

Nieuport 21 NR-3 of Lt Aleksandr N P de Seversky, 2nd Naval Fighter Detachment, Riga, Russia, October 1917

Moving on to flying a land-based Nieuport 21 – essentially a Nieuport 17 with the 110 hp Le Rhône rotary engine replaced by a retrograde 80 hp Le Rhône – Seversky scored his fifth and sixth victories on 10 October 1917. A similar aeroplane, bearing the tactical number NR-1, was flown by Lt Mikhail I Safanov as commander of the 2nd Land Detachment of the 2nd Air Division at Kuivastoin. He used the Nieuport to down aeroplanes on 7 September and 16 and 17 November 1917.

17

Shchetinin M-15 NR-2 of Lt Mikhail I Safanov, 1st Air Detachment 'Glagol', 2nd Air Division, Kuivastoin, Russia, July 1917

Mikhail Safanov had scored his first victory in M-9 NR-29, armed with a Madsen machine gun, on 9 September 1916. Promoted to lieutenant on 10 July 1917, he was piloting this M-15 (a smaller version of the M-9) on 14 July when he intercepted a German aeroplane approaching Arensburg and, after firing on it from a distance of 100 metres, saw it descend. Although nobody saw his foe crash, Safanov was credited with his second victory.

18

Lohner Type M L16 of Lschlt Gottfried Banfield,
***Seeflugstation* Trieste, Italy, August 1916**
First flying in L16 on 5 April 1916, Banfield bolted an 8 mm Schwarzlose MG 07/12 machine gun to the hull of the flying boat and flew it as a single-seater, scoring five victories between 23 June and 15 August. His success influenced the emergence of a brief vogue in flying boat fighters on both sides of the Adriatic.

19

Oeffag Type H A11 of Lschlt Gottfried Banfield,
***Seeflugstation* Trieste, Italy, August 1917**
Designed by Josef Mickl specifically for Banfield, the Oeffag Type H was powered by a 200 hp Hiero engine and mounted two Schwarzlose MG 07/12 machine guns. Banfield painted the flying boat blue to camouflage it against the sea and the night sky. At 2330 hrs on 31 May 1917 he used it to shoot a flying boat down near the mouth of the Primero River. The Italians towed the aeroplane back to Grado the next morning. This, his ninth confirmed victory, was also the first achieved by an Austro-Hungarian pilot at night. Declaring A11 his favourite aeroplane, Banfield said 'it was so good that I repeatedly suggested that it be built in quantity, but this was never done'.

20

Lohner Type TL L131 of Frglt Friedrich Lang and Stabsmaschinenwärter Franz Kohlhauser, *Seeflugstation* Durazzo, Albania, August 1916
Lohner TLs L120 to L139 were licence-built in Budapest by the Ungarische Flugzeugfabrik AG, using uprated 175 hp Rapp Rp III engines in lieu of the original 160 hp Mercedes D IIIs. On 22 August 1916 Lang scored his first two victories in concert with his observer, Kohlhauser, in a running fight near the Skumbi Estuary, off the Albanian coast, with Farmans of Italian *34ª Squadriglia*. These were also apparently among five credited to Zugsführer Julius Arigi and Fw Johann Lasi of *Flik* 6.

21

Phönix D I A115 of Frglt Friedrich Lang, Altura, Croatia, May 1918
Part of a naval detachment of Phönix D Is stationed at Altura aerodrome, near Pola naval base, A115 was flown by Lang on 19 May 1918 when he and three comrades downed two Macchi M.5s of *261ª Squadriglia*. One crashed in flames while the other M.5, M7280 flown by Tenente di Vascello Umberto Magaldi, was found drifting 17 miles west of Rovigno by *Tb 81*, which captured the pilot and sank the flying boat. Three days later Lang in A110 and Frglt Stefan Wollemann in A115 took on two M.5s flown by Tenente di Vascello Orazio Pierozzi and 2º Nocciere Beniamino Piro of *260ª Squadriglia* off Rovigno. This time the Macchis fared remarkably well, with Pierozzi claiming probable hits on one antagonist, which in this instance turned out to be an understatement – the wounded Wollemann ditched A115 just short of Pola.

22

FBA Type H No 414(?) of Tenente di Vascello Orazio Pierozzi and Ercole Bellingeri, *255ª Squadriglia*, Brindisi, Italy, May 1917
Pierozzi was photographed in this SIAI-built FBA, and it is known to have been on the *255ª Squadriglia* rolls as late as 28 August 1917, when it suffered a damaging crash. Based on that circumstantial evidence, the flying boat is reconstructed as it would probably have looked when Pierozzi scored his first confirmed victory on 7 June 1917, with roundels added in accordance with marking practice as of October 1916, and bearing the black pennant number 14, with no squadron marking in accordance with policy at the Brindisi Seaplane Station. Pierozzi went on to score six more victories in M.5 M7256, pennant No 18, while leading the Italian flying boat fighters from Venice in 1918.

23

Macchi M.5 M7242 of Tenente di Vascello Federico C Martinengo, *260ª Squadriglia*, Sant' Andrea, Italy, Spring 1918.
Commanding *260ª Squadriglia* from December 1917 to June 1918, Federico Martinengo marked his M.5 with alternating green and red bands and the number '1', along with the personal touch of a winged, pot-bellied rat.

24

Macchi M.5 M7289 of Sottotenente di Vascello Umberto Calvello, *260ª Squadriglia*, Sant' Andrea, Italy, Spring 1918
Calvello usually flew M 5 No 2, whose hull he decorated with *Fortunello*, an Italian cartoon character based on Frederick Burr Opper's popular American comic strip *The Happy Hooligan*. Depicted in an uncharacteristically aggressive attitude to match that of Calvello himself, Fortunello shouts in Venetian dialect, *'Ocio! Ocio! Fiol d'un Can!'* ('Look out! Look out! Son of a bitch!'), while his suitcase bears the legend *'Marciare non marcire'* ('March, don't rot').

25

Macchi M.5 M7229 of Landsman for Quartermaster Charles H Hammann, USNAS Porto Corsini, Italy, August 1918
Charles Hazeltine Hammann's Macchi is shown in standard livery, as was common on most newly delivered aircraft at USNAS Porto Corsini in the summer of 1918 – more distinctive markings appeared later. During a fight between four M.5s and five Phönix D Is on 21 August 1918, Ens George M Ludlow's M.5, M13015, was shot down with a smashed magneto and a punctured radiator and crankcase just five miles from the enemy naval base at Pola, but Hammann landed his own damaged Macchi alongside to rescue Ludlow. For that deed, Hammann became the first American to earn the Medal of Honor for courage above and beyond the call of duty in aerial combat. Tragically, he died in a post-war air crash in Langley, Virginia, on 21 June 1919.

26

Sopwith Camel B6338 of Lt Cdr Aristeides Moraitinis, squadron H2, Mudros, Lemnos, October 1918
Powered by a Clerget 9B rotary engine, Clayton &

Shuttleworth-built Camel B6338 is known to have been assigned to 2 Naval Wing on 9 October 1917, flying from Mudros through to 1 December. It was at Imbros in March 1918, suggesting that it may have spent the past several months being flown by the Greeks of Z Sqn, quite possibly including Lt Cdr Aristeides Moraitinis. It was at the Mudros repair base in June and officially assigned to the Royal Hellenic Navy in October 1918. In an order dated 28 August 1917, Greek marking policy specified roundels in the blue and white national colours on the wings and fuselage, while retaining the blue, white and red bands of the 'Entente powers' on the rudders. Photographic evidence, however, suggests that in practice Squadron H2's Camels retained all their original British markings, at least until the end of the war.

27
de Havilland DH 9 E8991 of Capt Aristeides Moraitinis, squadron H2, Mudros, Lemnos, November 1918
At war's end the British delivered three DH 9s to the Royal Hellenic forces, of which E8991 was presented to Capt Moraitinis. The aeroplane boasted a small plaque that read 'To the Commander A Moraitinis, DSO'.

28
Sopwith Camel D9649 of Lt(jg) David S Ingalls, No 213 Sqn, Bergues, France, September 1918
No photograph has yet turned up of any of David Ingalls' Camels, and the author's inquiries on how they were finished elicited a response of 'plain' from the US Navy's first ace. Such illustrations as have been made – including one by a contemporary that Ingalls knew, pilot and artist Clayton Knight – support the likelihood that, in a squadron with a different marking policy for each flight, Ingalls dispensed with anything beyond the serial number. He scored three of his victories in Clayton & Shuttleworth-built Camel D9649, which was also used by his flight leader, Capt Colin P Brown, to send a two-seater down out of control on 21 August 1918. Ingalls, in turn, flew Ruston & Proctor-built D8177 (which figured in seven of Brown's 14 victories) to down a Fokker D VII over Vlisseghem on 20 September.

BIBLIOGRAPHY

Bartlett, C P O, *Bomber Pilot – 1917-1918,* Ian Allan Ltd, Shepperton, Surrey, 1974

Christiansen, Friedrich, translated by O'Brien Browne, 'Battle Flights Over the Channel', *Over the Front,* Vol 15, No 3, Fall 2000, pp 231-232

Flanagan, Brian P, 'Emil Meinecke - Fighter Ace of the Dardanelles', *Cross & Cockade Journal* (USA), Vol 12, No 3, pp 244-248

Franks, Norman, Bailey, Frank and Duiven, Rick, *The Jasta War Chronology,* Grub Street, London, 1998

Franks, Norman, Bailey, Frank W and Guest, Russell, *Above the Lines,* Grub Street, London, 1993

Franks, Norman, *Bloody April . . . Black September,* Grub Street, London, 1995

Franks, Norman, *Osprey Aircraft of the Aces 67 - Sopwith Pup Aces of World War 1,* Osprey, Botley, Oxford, 2005

Franks, Norman, *Osprey Aircraft of the Aces 62 - Sopwith Triplane Aces of World War 1,* Osprey, Botley, Oxford, 2004

Gentilli, Roberto, Iozzi, Antonio and Varriale, Paolo, *Italian Aces of World War I and Their Aircraft,* Schiffer Publications, Atglen, Pennsylvania, 2003

Grosz, P M, *Windsock Datafile 25 - Fokker D VIII,* Albatross Productions, Ltd, Berkhamsted, Herts, 1991

Naval Aviation: A Personal History - A Weapon Tested, The Historical Archive, New Media LLC, 2008

Nicolle, David, 'Young Turks - Ottoman Turkish Fighters 1915-1918', *Air Enthusiast No 74,* March/April 1998, pp 44-45

Olynyk, Frank J, 'David Ingalls, United States Naval Reserve Flying Corps', *Cross & Cockade Journal* (USA), Vol 22, No 2, pp 97-121

O'Neal, Michael, 'Madison Ace - Lt Kenneth Unger', *Over the Front,* Vol 14, No 3, Fall 1999

Paloubis, Ioannis, *From the Seas . . . To the Skies, The Naval Air Force Chronicle, 1913-1941,* Hellenic Maritime Museum, Piraeus, Greece, 2009

Pieters, Walter M, *The Belgian Air Service in the First World War,* Aeronaut Books, Indio, California, 2010

Puglisi, William R, 'Jacobs of *Jasta* 7 - Highest Ranking Living German Aces of World War I', *Cross & Cockade Journal* (USA), Vol 6, No 4, pp 307-327

Rossano, Geoffrey L, ed, *The Price of Honor - The World War One Letters of Naval Aviator Kenneth MacLeish,* Naval Institute Press, Annapolis, Maryland, 1991

Schmeelke, Michael, translated by Adam Wait, "'Flugobermatros Friedrich Gröschke'", *Over the Front,* Vol 7, No 3, pp 256-263

Shores, Christopher, Franks, Norman and Guest, Russell, *Above the Trenches,* Grub Street, London, 1990

Skelton, Marvin L, annotator and editor, 'Frank A Dixon And The 17th Aero Squadron', *Cross & Cockade Journal* (USA), Vol 19, No 2, p 166

Stormer, Dr Fritz, translated by Peter Kilduff, 'Seaplanes in Combat', *Cross & Cockade (USA) Journal,* Vol 20, No 2, pp 110, 119-120 and 125

Taylor, Stewart K, 'Down but Not Necessarily Out', *Over the Front,* Vol 21, No 1, Spring 2006, pp 53-73

Wright, Peter, 'Chippy's Aviator - Herbert Rutter Simms', *Cross & Cockade Journal (Great Britain),* Vol 13, No 3, pp 121-122

INDEX

References to illustrations are shown in **bold**. Plates are shown with page and caption locators in brackets.